Robert [illegible]
1966

The Church is Different

by ROBERT ADOLFS O.S.A.

Translated by HUBERT HOSKINS

HARPER & ROW, PUBLISHERS

New York

2101

Nihil obstat: Raphael Kuiters, O.S.A., Censor Deputatus; Imprimi permittimus: Lucas Hoogveld, O.S.A., Prior Provincialis; Imprimatur: Mathew A. P. J. Oomens, Vic. gen. Diocesis Buscoducensis.

FIRST EDITION

LIBRARY OF CONGRESS CATALOG CARD NUMBER: 66-15862

Contents

Introduction

For some this is a time of fearful confusion; for others one of great, perhaps exhilarating, expectations. The one Christian is beset with anxiety because the citadel of his churchly life and allegiance has begun to crumble—or so it would seem—and those parts of the structure that he firmly believed to be inviolable begin to look as though they may not be so irreplaceable, after all. Not yet given over to uttering cries of despair, he none the less fears for the future.

For another Christian, however, it is as if a burden had fallen from his shoulders. He is glad to feel about him an atmosphere of freedom. He has room to breathe. He is fascinated by the splendour and allure of the wide open spaces.

When a Church has existed over many centuries in an enclosed atmosphere and the individual Christian has lived all too long in the imagined security of structures and formulas passed on and accepted without any radical questioning, it is inevitable that finding himself suddenly out in the open, the one man will run for shelter, while the other experiences a kind of intoxication.

The man seized with agoraphobia is not to be abandoned to his own devices; nor are we simply to commiserate with him. The call of the wide open spaces is indeed a call—and one that requires us to have an attentive and receptive mind for *what is in store for us*, a responsible care for the Church of the future.

To which I would add that just to stagger around in a newly won openness and freedom can blind us to the fact that Christianity—and consequently the Church—is in the throes of a grave crisis which mere openness will not, of itself, help us to surmount. It can only lead to a wild and irresponsible hunt after novelty for its own sake, to a loose experimentation and an attitude of intolerance towards those who are more conservatively inclined. What is needed is the effort to think and act in a responsible, fresh and profoundly creative way. We must in all conscience try to discover an authentically religious inspiration, at the same time looking out for the forms in which this inspiration might be cast. Nothing would be more disastrous for a genuine, evolutive renewal of the Church and of Christianity than an attitude rooted in the conviction that, of course, we know already in which direction the Spirit is taking us. I, for one, make no claim to such knowledge; but I am ready to seek and to knock, and so to persist in the hope that he who seeks will find, and to him that knocks it shall be opened.

Over the past centuries Christianity and the Church have developed, certainly; but they have done so within static structures which allowed no room for a radical change of course or for rapid adjustment to new circumstances. And all of a sudden we find ourselves caught up in a torrent, in a process of acceleration of which the end is not in sight.

Perhaps, though, we have been too sure of ourselves and of what it is we should be up to. In our dogmatic formulas we have *possessed ourselves*—as we supposed—of the Christian revelation; and we have indulged the illusion that the Church of Christ was firmly anchored and grounded in ecclesial structures, safeguarded by a highly centralized governmental machine. Perhaps what we possessed was a collective ecclesiastical consciousness—assured, reassuring and triumphalist; but what we lacked was the holy fire of a real faith.

Unconsciously, almost, we lived by the notion that Christianity—and therefore the Church as well—despite the stresses and strains of the passing years, had a fixed abode within this world, that nothing could violate or destroy. Development and adjustment, of course, there had to be; but these related to secondary, rather unimportant, issues, and to nothing more. Any new errors had to be nosed out and condemned, naturally; and it went without saying that on dangerous political tendencies and ideological views of life and the world the Church must make her attitude crystal clear. All dogmatic tenets—such as, for example, the Trinity and Christology—had been brought under discussion, for the most part with a view to discrediting this or that heretic. In substance, at any rate, the content, formulation and framework of these dogmas had been settled; and only with respect to certain incidentals was it still possible to make a few finer distinctions here and there. In our own day the last remaining tractates of theology—Mariology and eschatology—have come up in their turn. Apparently, in these areas of doctrine some development was still feasible.[1] In the moral sphere, certain questions—having to do, chiefly, with marital ethics—still presented some difficulties; but the basic principles were assured. So too, of course, was natural law. It was simply a matter of making the right deductions and applying them intelligently; and of course there was always an absolute guarantee—the infallible magisterium—available to ensure that it would be done correctly. There again, the Church was bound to set her face against a mounting secularization and against materialism—two dangers which beset modern society through developments in the technical and scientific sphere. What has called a halt to these more or less consciously articulated ideas, with their strong suggestion of a complacent, "bourgeois" mentality, is the course events have taken during these last few years—in particular, the challenge voiced by Pope John and the fact of the Council.[1]

And so the thought is slowly seeping through that two thousand years of Christianity do not guarantee a well-established, solidly structured Church or an ensconced, nicely defined and circumscribed Christian religion. No. Indeed, one may begin to suspect that we have scarcely come to terms, as yet, with the essential problems—and this is especially true of the problem presented by the Church herself. One of the major questions is the *catholicity* of the Church; and that is the subject of this book.

Now that I have finished it, I realize just how many people

[1] It should be noted that this book was written while the Council was still in progress.—*Trans.*

in fact have helped to bring this work to fruition. I am particularly indebted to my fellow Augustinians, for their conversations with me and also for the encouragement they have given me. I am grateful also to those with whom it has been given to me to discuss these matters in ecumenical groups and elsewhere, and for the stimulus afforded by the Catholic Circle and the many conversations I have enjoyed with the students of the Technical College at Eindhoven.

I

True Catholicity

The evolution of the concept "catholicity"

"I believe in one, holy, catholic and apostolic Church"—so runs the Creed which we affirm. What this means, first of all, is that the Church is for us an object of faith; but it means too that these four notes and properties of the Church are part of the faith, part of what we believe.

In denoting the Church we have given the term "catholic" pride of place, as if to say that what primarily characterizes the Church is, of course, her catholicity. The Church of Christ is the Church that has the right to call herself "catholic", that is, the Church universal, the Church overall. Now the thing to note is that this catholicity did not become manifest all at once. No doubt the idea itself is present in the Bible; the word "catholic" is not.

In order to bring out the privileged position enjoyed by Jewry, Christ at first says that he has been sent to the sheep of the house of Israel. When that people's obduracy has become apparent, the Lord charges the Apostles—immediately prior to his ascension—with the task of universal proclamation (Matt. 28. 19)—but even then in such a way that the Gospel is to be preached first to Israel. As the proclamation to the Jews has only a very modest success, Paul addresses his preaching to the Gentiles; and it is revealed to Peter that he is to receive them into the Church without requiring them to conform to the Jewish law. After James's martyrdom and Peter's arrest (Acts 12. 1–17), the Gospel is preached—mainly at the instance of Paul—to the Gentiles. Even Paul usually still preaches first of all in the Jewish synagogue; but as hope of converting the Israelites dwindles, Paul again takes the lead in stressing the complete equality of all men in Christ (Eph. 2. 11–3. 7).

In a sense, Paul is the theologian from whom catholicity acquired a deeper significance. In his Letter to the Ephesians he speaks of the mystery that embraces the whole content and meaning of revelation: God has made known to us his secret counsel, "the mystery of his will", the decision he had taken in Christ, when the fullness of time should come, *to unite all things* in Christ (Eph. 1. 9–10). As man within his cosmic setting had become disintegrated and therefore divided and estranged from his fellows, so the mighty work of Christ was to make all things and all men *one* again, to bring them under *one* Head in him.

This reuniting, this calling men together *(ek-klesis)* to unity in Christ, has been, since the first Pentecost and through the operation of God's Spirit, the business of the Church. Indeed one might say that basically the Church *is* that reuniting of all human beings, peoples and cultures. *Thus the Church is universal, is all-embracing, is that which brings all things together in a single whole.* That is the idea which for Paul provides the ground and basis for the catholicity of the Church. Again, it is at once evident that catholicity goes hand in hand, so to speak, with that other hallmark of the Church: her unity.[1]

So it is that at about the turn of the first century we find the thing I have just been describing expressed by the Greek term *kata holon*. It was the bishop and martyr, Ignatius of Antioch, who first used this expression: "Where Jesus Christ is, there is the *catholic* Church." The Church Fathers, Augustine in particular, were to give the term "catholic" an implication even more profound.

It has been a tradition among theologians to speak of an external and an internal or interior catholicity.[2] External catholicity signifies that the Church of Christ is meant for the whole world, for all races and indeed for the men of every time and place. Interior catholicity implies that Christ has proclaimed the fullness of truth to his

Church and has endowed her with every good and perfect gift.

The Church as an "eventualizing"

The idea abovementioned is one to which we can subscribe; but the trouble starts when one begins to realize how the Church in her self-awareness has understood this "catholicity". A theology infected with a static type of conceptualizing has imposed on the idea of "catholicity" a triumphalist interpretation; and this in turn arises from the way in which the Church has been envisaged—in Roman Catholic theology—as a static, realized entity, a house ready and occupied, which can only become "more full" (quantitative expansion) and possesses already the fullness of revelation and of every saving benefit—a possession that can only be entered into more deeply and in certain incidental respects further opened to the view (expansion as a process of making explicit).

Any conceptual system, however, which is static in character is essentially inadequate. It cannot possibly do justice to the range and depth of what the Church means and is. The Church is an event, a process in which people are called together by the Spirit—people who acknowledge and confess Christ as their redeemer. When people are united in this way, however, this is something living; and therefore it partakes of, and is subject to, the dynamic character of all living things. That is why the Church is to be envisaged first and foremost as *event* and not as an in essence already complete, realized entity which has, so to speak, appropriated all its assets. The Church is a continuing event that is being accomplished in history and *through* people. The being-called-together of people under Christ as the one Head (Eph. 1. 9.)—that in essence is the Church. But it is not something signed, sealed and delivered to us by God; rather is it—for all who belong to such a Church—*a continuing task*. The notion is a paradoxical one: that "to be the Church" is itself a continuing charge which Christ lays upon his Church.

If then the Church is primarily a process going on in history and is also a permanent charge, this means that unity and catholicity are not qualities which she possesses *a priori*; they have a real being in the Church *as that with which she is charged, not as something fully and finally given, but as that which she is given to achieve*. This is strikingly put—although perhaps not radically enough—by Laurentius Klein: "Now it is important to see—what indeed on our part has been all too little emphasized—that these four marks of the Church are not simply 'attributes', but also an imperative commission. They carry with them the command to bring about what Christ has thereby given to us. In contemporary terms it means something like this: Christ has established his Church as one, holy, catholic and apostolic; and it is our job to put all this into action (by his grace), that is, to turn the Church into event, to make it happen."[3]

We are charged with—among other things—realizing unity and catholicity, so that the Church may "occur"; in other words, we are to make the Church come about.

It is remarkable how in his parables of the Kingdom (of which the Church is the initial stage) Christ invariably uses images which are *dynamic*. Most striking is that of the mustard-seed, and again that of the yeast or leaven (Matt. 13. 31–34). In both these parables the salient features are clearly those of growth, of development, of a vital *process* for which *time* is requisite: "it is the smallest of all seeds, but when it has grown . . ."; and "the Kingdom of heaven is like leaven which a woman took and hid in three measures of meal, till it was all leavened".[4]

We can say that in the kernel the mustard-seed already *is*, and already contains, the full-grown tree in which the birds of the air make their nest. What there is in *fact* is scarcely anything at all: an unprepossessing little seed that must first be planted and take root, and then by a process of fertilization and growth become the "actual thing", namely, a large tree. To this tiny mustard-seed we may compare the Church as a growth towards the fulfilment of the Kingdom of God.

Christ is the sower: "He who sows the good seed is the Son of Man" (Matt. 13. 37). Ours is the obligation to make the *hidden promises* which this seed enfolds come to fruition. Our task, then, is described in the application of the parable of the sower as: to heed (be receptive to), to understand, to accept, to put down roots and to fructify.

We can now raise the question: is the Church already there? Or: is there already such a thing as the Church? The impression we get is that this question has nearly always been answered with an unqualified "yes". The Church, it was said, is already there; and this Church, which exists already, can only be rendered more explicit, is open simply to quantitative enlargement. But such an answer fails to do justice to the parable of the seed. We are not one hundred per cent receptive of the seed. Even we Christians prove sometimes to be "the wayside", even we are sometimes stony ground, even we have thistles enough to stunt and choke—whether in whole or in part—what God has given. I would want at this point to say that *the* Church does not yet exist, but that *to a limited degree it is being actualized*. In other words, it is certain that we are a long way still from having realized in fact all the potentialities of the Church. We can get some idea of this if we try to imagine what might have happened if the Church had not expanded in a westerly direction but had reached its major development *first* in the East, among the Asian peoples; or if there had been no split in the Roman Empire during the ninth century, and consequently no rift in the Church; or if Augustine's writings had all been destroyed; or again, if there had been no Donatists and no Pelagians. Every turning-point in the Church's history is ambiguous: on the one hand it has meant a particular development—often enough a rich and rewarding one—in a direction determined by this or that turn of history; while on the other, the consequence has been that certain very definite possibilities have been not only unrealized but often no longer perceived, so far as the Church is concerned.

We have not the faintest idea what seed the Son of Man

has yet in store, in the way of potentialities and resources still undeveloped. To take as one's standpoint the idea that the Church already, in all actuality, *is*—even granting that the Church can, of course, be "adapted", renewed, rejuvenated, expanded and better structured—is to be blind to our sinful barrenness or to our human limitations, which have prevented all sorts of as yet unknown possibilities in the Church from coming to growth and bearing fruit. As we have already said, therefore, we have to become aware once more of our responsibility for what is coming in our day; in other words, our vital need is to be attentive and receptive and open to what is on the way.

These are the things we must keep in view every time we talk here about *the Church as a task* and a charge, and when we say that our continuing task is to make the Church and all her potentialities come about.

It is my conviction that the smallmindedness, impotence and guilt of us men have in the course of the centuries had a more and more limiting and constricting effect on, for instance, the injunction regarding the catholicity of the Church (a matter taken up in the next chapter). This does not discredit, *per se*, the realization of the Church as we find it at the moment; for human smallmindedness, sin and shortcoming are intrinsic to the form in which the Church is concretely manifested. It is, after all, a Church of sinners.

But the situation becomes really critical when the Church, no longer conscious of her shortcomings, *forgets* her essential obligations and takes shelter behind this or that triumphalist slogan (as, for example: "we *are* the one, true Church", rather than: "we have the solemn obligation to be the one, true Church"). The Church is then a venerable but ossified museum-piece, and no longer in any real sense a "happening". She becomes a House well and truly built, indeed; but is she also one in which the Man who had nowhere to lay his head can dwell?

Too much of the institution and too little charisma, law exploiting and overriding love, the "frozen" rest of the possessor where there ought to be that abiding unrest which Christ's command must always arouse—these all typify the crisis of this moment.

Yet it is also a moment of hope—and in that we live. "We must learn to hope again," says Ernest Bloch; and perhaps we are beginning to learn just that. There was more to the mind of faith in the fellowship of the Church—it now appears—than we had suspected. And when the "hope of new life for the Church" burst upon the Council we were dumbstruck.

Catholicity and Council

Without being pretentious, I want to try and turn the spotlight on to catholicity, the idea and the actuality, its possible implications and those aspects of it which remain unrealized. It is an outstanding feature of the Council that it has already enriched, and given greater depth to, the idea of catholicity. I have in mind here not so much the speeches and deliverances of the bishops as the novel and all but imperceptible way in which the conciliar gathering came to understand itself.

In the past, Councils have been primarily "domestic" events: that is, they were in the final instance concerned with regulating the internal affairs of the Church and of the ecclesial community. Earlier Councils addressed themselves primarily to the Church's members, to the faithful, over whom the Fathers of the Council exercised control. One has to view their pronouncements in that light, in order to understand their proper place and significance. This sort of condemnation loomed large at the earlier Councils in view of the fact that a Council's business was usually and for the most part to pronounce upon those trends of thought and action within the Church community which—after due examination—appeared to be a danger to the faith or even to contradict it. In short, former Councils have been paramountly domestic occasions. Their outreach extended no further than to the community of the Church—a community that was a world apart, as it were, homogeneous and, in one sense, isolated from the rest of mankind.

The Church is Different

It has gradually become clear that a Church separated off from the rest of the world represents an outmoded situation. In a world striving with unprecedented vigour and determination after unity a Church can no longer be a world apart, or a Council any longer a purely domestic event within such a Church. It is that too, of course: an event, a "happening" of the Church and in the Church. But there can be no doubt that in this age the Council has become a world event by force of circumstances, as it were. Willy-nilly, the Council is now addressing itself no longer simply to the faithful of the Church but to the world as well—the Christian world and the non-Christian world, the world of believers and the atheist world too. At all events, the importance attached to the Council by non-Catholics in general is very considerable indeed.[5]

In a perspective of this sort a condemnation, for instance, of atheism, or of any other movements and tendencies more or less inimical to belief, is, if not senseless, at any rate extremely ambiguous. The truth is that any such pronouncement would either speak to Christians alone—in which case it has no point—or it is meant for the whole world of unbelief; but then there is the risk that such a measure might prove something of a boomerang.

The Church must not condemn (in the old sense of the word) those who are unbelievers; but she has the duty to proclaim to them the *Glad Tidings*. To speak of "Tidings" is to speak of "dialogue", and thus of encounter with many people and groupings of widely diverse character. The aim of such encounter is for each to understand, to listen and above all to give himself, to the other. To every dialogue there is a dimension of listening and a dimension of giving. Seen from this standpoint, a blanket condemnation of everything and everybody outside the Christian world puts an end to any possibility of dialogue.

The Church has no duty to isolate herself from the world; but she does have a gift for that world. Yet giving is itself an impossibility without a readiness to listen and receive; and this receptivity again cannot exist apart from a humble awareness that the world in its turn has something to give the Church. The gulf between Church and world can only be increased, so long as the Church gives the impression that the power to run the whole show, unbelievers included, is really hers, and that it is up to her to decide what those who are not members of the Church at all are to think and do.

For the most part, of course, the Church will not pass judgment on unbelievers as individual people; but principally she condemns those philosophical, economic and political currents and systems (Marxism, for instance, and existentialism) which are more or less tied in with atheism or with other non-Christian and sceptical tendencies. There is then a considerable risk, though, that this will make confusion worse confounded. Socialism and Marxism—let alone existentialism—are not just repudiations of God. All these schools and systems of thought contain what are often extremely highminded ideas and positive values; and it is bound to be dangerous to lump them all together indiscriminately and condemn the whole lot out of hand.

The two dimensions of catholicity

Catholicity is a universalism—but not a totalitarian one, not a "universalism of power", that would dictate to the whole world how and what it must think and do. Catholicity here has two dimensions. The first is *breadth*: it is a geographical, surface dimension—literally and figuratively; and it means that the Church unites in herself people from every part of the world. The fact that the bishops came together at the Council from all over the world was eloquent witness to this aspect of catholicity.

Traditional ways of thinking about the Church's universalism have often over-valued this dimension. It is splendid, of course, to be able to show, with figures and maps and so forth, how big and strong the Catholic Church is in so many parts of the world. But what the figures and the maps may obscure is the major problem of the missionary enterprise today: the baptismal water flows in abundance over bodies, it is true; but does it seep through into hearts and minds? Mission will soon find itself in a serious impasse, unless it makes the effort to penetrate into men's thoughts and lives and forms of culture, however primitive or however highly developed these may be.

Not long ago a certain religious order undertook to set up a seminary for the training of native clergy in Nairobi. Immediately, an appeal was made to their colleagues in Europe to collect and send out a number of copies of an extremely antiquated handbook on Aristotelean-Thomistic philosophy. Does Christianity, then, really have to be brought to non-Westerners via the rigid Latin formulas of an otherwise pretty desiccated kind of Western thinking?

That is why we are anxious to drive home the importance of the much neglected *depth-dimension* of catholicity. Above and before everything else, this has to do with a universalism of love—of a Christian love that takes into itself and makes its own a concern for the whole of mankind. That Catholicism is truly "catholic" which shares in the life of man as man, accepts its part in his fear and suffering—a Catholicism which is flexible and adapts to the needs of contemporary man, of this man who may indeed be looking to atheism, humanism or existentialism to save and deliver him. The Church is truly "catholic" if and when she takes contemporary man—whoever he may be—seriously. And that can only be done through dialogue, by adopting towards the world and modern man an attitude of willingness to listen and receive.

There is a second aspect of the depth-dimension; and it refers to the way a true catholicity adapts and integrates with itself everything of positive value in different cultures, in leading schools of thought and in the various movements of the mind and spirit. Even in the past the Church has done this. She assimilated what was of value in the Platonic world of thought and later made herself conversant with Aristotelean thinking, so as to construct within them a magnificent synthesis of the Christian faith. In a way that one can only admire, the Church managed to integrate into her liturgy Roman cultus and Roman forms of culture; she was incarnated in the political system of the Roman Empire and has applied certain elements of it to her own ecclesial structure. All of this becomes really problematical as soon as the culture, the world of thought and the political system vanish, while the Church goes on clinging to what had long ago been commandeered from cultures and worlds now outmoded, and invests these things with a quasi-divine origin. Then the Church loses contact with the mental outlook and temper prevailing at a given moment in history. She becomes immobile, fixed rigidly in forms within which the religious inspiration peculiar to the time can no longer find an outlet.

Naturally, this aspect of the depth-dimension of catholicity has its risks to run. The Church has had to contend in earlier times with such difficulties. There is always the danger that the Church as a community, instead of adapting and integrating a particular culture and thought-world on Christian lines, will be overwhelmed by them and absorbed into them. But these are simply the dangers of living, in all its forms. The principle of the incarnation implies that the Church enter into each phase of history and every available form of human existence in order to really *live* in it, not as a closed and segregated sect but as an integral part of a living world.

The risks conceded, must we not say nevertheless that it is far more dangerous to incarcerate oneself in, for instance, typically Western forms of culture and ways of thought and then to absolutize these as *the* Catholic *modus vivendi*? The silly stampede for total security, and alarm at whatever seems strange simply because it is "different", have served the Church an ill turn and done serious harm to her catholicity. I somehow have the feeling that Augustine was more catholic than we are now; indeed, it was Augustine who ventured to take in Jeremiah and Plato, Paul and Plotinus, John and Origen, Cyprian and Athanasius, and to make them all part and parcel of his theology and pastoralia. It is not for the Church just to *try* and be Catholic in this way or merely to condescend to "have a go"—it is her bounden duty and vocation.

It is the depth-dimension of catholicity in particular for which an attitude of openness, of willingness to listen and enter into dialogue, is in a special degree prerequisite. The principle was nicely put not very long ago by Pope Paul VI, when the Secretariat for Relations with the Non-Christian Religions was being instituted. It runs as follows: "The Church wishes to open up a respectful, two-way conversation with all peoples, all forms of modern life, all varieties of social and political expression, as are ready for such a dialogue on a basis of complete frankness and genuine humanity" (sermon during Pontifical High Mass in St Peter's, Easter 1964).

The phrase "an open catholicism" has been known to be employed in this connection. As it stands, it is a somewhat peculiar expression. If "catholicism" here be taken to refer to a certain mode of existence evinced by the Roman Catholic Church, then one might understand it in this sense: that in the course of its history Catholicism has manifested itself now as "closed" and now again as "open". If one brings the term "catholicity" into it, the expression ceases to mean anything. An "open catholicity" is tautological; and a "closed catholicity" is no catholicity at all.

In what follows we shall take "open catholicism" as referring to the depth-dimension of catholicity; and we shall seek to establish what some, at any rate, of its implications are. The openness must be taken to apply inside as well as outside the Church—hence a chapter on this aspect of catholicity. The need for openness in theology is demonstrated chiefly by reference to the impasse prevailing in the moral sector. What "catholicity" might mean in the basically dialogical approach to a non-Catholic contemporary world movement is suggested in what is said about the Church and communism in Chapter VII. That a real catholicity needs to be geared quite differently again, when it comes to relations with the churches of the Reformation and the ecumenical movement generally, is a further issue that must necessarily be taken into account (see Chapter VI).

Modernism and German Catholicism during the Nazi period each have a separate section to themselves, because they afford the most grievous—and indeed not so distant—example of the fatal consequences of a "closed catholicism" or of a catholicity forgetful of its depth-dimension. But our first task is to show how in the course of the centuries catholicity became increasingly cabin'd, cribb'd and confined.

II

Between Integralism and Catholicity

The catholic character of Christianity is always being threatened by forces tending to hem it in or to separate it off. And so the history of the Church is rather like the movement of a pendulum swinging between universalism and integralism. Over and over again, you get "elite" groups springing up—and these can be whole areas of culture—which cut themselves off and claim that they and they alone practise the "real" Christian way of life, or simply that they are "the" Christians, they *are* Christendom.[1] This is plainly a negativizing outlook that runs clean against any sort of authentic catholicity. Yet this is by no means always obvious—especially if your standpoint happens to be that of such an exclusivist group, and you take it all for granted.

It is this tendency—opposed to a Christian universalism—that we wish to denote from now on when we speak of *integralism*. We shall understand, then, by that term the more or less organized, or unquestioningly accepted, closed, sectarian Christian grouping which bases its existence on the belief that it possesses an absolute, or at any rate more sublime, truth and for that reason separates itself off from the greater whole of society. This kind of "elite" group despises "the others", pushes them out, attacks them, tries to get the upper hand over them, or simply ignores them altogether.

The beginning of this century saw the growth of a well organized, fascist-like movement within the Church—one that was, as a matter of fact, called integralism. It was this that, especially during the pontificate of Pius X, operated in the Church as a "shadow government" behind the pope's back—and did so in a most destructive fashion. We shall have more to say about that in Section III of this chapter. First, however, we would like to call attention to some of the moments in the Church's history when integralism was particularly rife. In so doing, we cannot avoid the impression that in its movement between universalism and integralism the pendulum has swung more and more in the direction of a constricted and emaciated form of catholicity.

On the other hand, we believe that just now we have reached a turning-point, and that the Church is seriously trying to make good the damage to her catholicity: in other words, the whole movement of renewal within the Church has sprung from an irrepressible urge to be truly "catholic" again—and to be so in the most splendid and impressive way.

I. The Mounting Toll taken of Catholicity

It could be argued that there were integralist tendencies as early as the Apostolic and post-Apostolic period. The strain and stress between Jewish and Gentile Christians, gnosticism with its claims to a superior kind of spiritual knowledge, the parties that according to the First Letter to the Corinthians were fighting for a predominant place in the local community—all are instances of this. But when we speak of a progressive loss of catholicity, it is events on a much grander scale that we are thinking of. The first major retrenchment of Christian universalism came about in 1054. To get a proper grasp of what happened, we need to trace the course of events leading up to the fateful division between an Eastern and a Western Christianity; for the curious thing about it is that the basis for this historic inroad into catholicity was in part provided by what to start with had been a rapid expansion of Christianity—an expansion which at one time had appeared to bear a universalistic stamp.

The Constantinian turning-point

With the Emperor Constantine's conversion and the Edict of Milan in the year 313 the Church, which up to that moment had been persecuted, suddenly found that it had acquired a legal status within the Roman Imperium. After that, it did not take long for Christianity to become not just a tolerated religion but a religion of the State. Certain Protestant scholars in particular—Von Harnack, for example—have seen in this what they regard as a perversion of Christianity; by which they mean that the imperialistic proclivities of the Roman Empire then penetrated the Church for good and all. Although there is some truth in this view, it ignores an essential aspect of catholicity : to wit, that it is by its very nature *incarnational*. The incarnation is not apprehended in a proper "catholic" fashion, so long as we take it to refer merely to God's entry into history through the manhood of Christ; for that event must be extended to include Christianity itself—a Christianity which incarnates it in every historical situation.

It would be illogical, therefore, to expect of Christianity that in a world moulded to a rigid and systematized power structure it should or could continue to be a current of pure spirituality, "alongside" history. Had the Church insisted on remaining a "church of martyrs", it is not unlikely that Christianity would have become an insignificant sect.[2]

However conducive to the spread of Christianity the Constantinian watershed may have been, it also housed a potential threat to the fullness of catholicity. When after Constantine, under the Emperor Theodosius, Christianity graduated from being a *religio licita* to being the exclusive State religion and State cult, "Christian" became synonymous with "citizen of the Empire"; and that implied the identification of Christianity with a measurable area of political power and cultural influence (the *oikoumene*). The people outside this area—the non-Christians—were *ipso facto* the political enemy. The logical outcome of this principle was manifest in missionizing activity, which almost invariably relied for its effectiveness on war or on the threat of force. It became common practice and remained so—unchallenged—until far into the Middle Ages. Thus Charlemagne "converted" the Saxons by overrunning their territory and reducing that Germanic tribe to subjection. It went quite unnoticed that in this way the content of the term "catholicity" was being reduced to geographical expansion by dint of incorporating peoples into the Empire. It says much in this connection that not until 1622 was a *church* missionary institution established (the *Congregatio de propaganda fide*).

Another thing that happened in consequence of the turn events had taken under Constantine was that the status, place and function of the clergy gradually changed. The Emperor Constantine reorganized the hierarchical structure of the Church on the pattern of the State hierarchy. Thus the patriarchs were put on a par with the four *praefecti*, and metropolitans with provincial governors; while bishops—especially later on, as a result of a degree of inadequacy in the sphere of local administration—also succeeded to important positions of worldly power. They acquired influential privileges and were even brought in to administer the law. All this made possible the growth of a political power vested in the bishops and popes. At the same time, the seed was planted which enabled the clerisy to develop into a self-insulated and superior power-group within the Church—a process that involved a certain demoting of the laity to the level of "second-class" Christians. This too implies a restricted conception of catholicity.

The breach in the Imperium

Gradually the Church outgrew her close attachment to the Constantinian Empire. She became a power able to set itself above both imperial and local rulers. It was not until the eleventh century, however, that the full consequences of this were realized.

Charlemagne laid permanent foundations for a self-dependent Europe. To that end he adopted the traditions and structures of the Roman Empire, in order to transplant them into a new whole that would embrace the Frankish and Germanic peoples. In so doing, however, he lost the *oikoumene* of the Roman Empire. For what he in fact created was a duplicate version of it; and this found its clearest expression when in the year 800 he had himself crowned in Rome as emperor of the Western half of the original Imperium.

Up to then, not one of the Germanic overlords had managed to get himself into such a position, equal to that of the emperor in Constantinople; and so for quite a time it remained possible to make it look as if there were still an *oikoumene* under the ruling authority of the emperor in the East, while in fact the partitioning of the realm had already taken place. It was some time before it came to be recognized in the East that a rival had appeared on the Western horizon—a ruler who was actually staking a claim to the imperial dignity and governmental powers. What was worse, it was evidently no longer feasible to repair the damage. There were now two imperial governments; and the unity of the Roman Empire had gone for good. The conflict, however, and the separation of West from East, had the most painful consequences for Christianity and the Church.

In the West it was the popes who could vindicate a claim to universal government within the old unity. By various measures of reform they still tried to reinstate the earlier *oikoumene*; but they were no longer effective in pressing home their claims to primacy beyond the Western Church. When the pope finally voiced his demands in explicit terms, this was taken to be a direct affront to the imperial Byzantine Church. In 1054 the drama reached its catastrophe: the pope anathematized the Eastern Church. The schism was now a hard fact.

This frightful damage done to the Church's unity came as a blow to the universality of the *Ecclesia Catholica*. It was not just a geographical and numerical retrenchment; but the depth-dimension of catholicity suffered immense hurt also. For all the riches of Eastern theology, devotion, cultic forms and religious inspiration ceased for the most part to have a fructifying effect upon the Church (of the

West). In recent years studies of the Christian East have served to reveal just how great this loss has been.

The Middle Ages

Medieval Christendom was an impressive whole. The Christians of that period saw the world as a "Christian world". Islam and paganism, even though sometimes felt to be a threat, were still regarded as more or less "fringe phenomena". Within this Christian world the two powers, of Empire and of Church, hold each other—not without upsets and disturbances—in equal check. State and Church, nature and culture, are adumbrations of the Kingdom of God. All earthly things are a symbol of things heavenly. The medieval world, therefore, is static and closed. Man lives in the consciousness of unity within a mighty circle which at the same time constitutes for all practical purposes the horizon of everything that has a real existence in this world. True, there are disquieting factors here and there, such as heresies and—on the outer edge—the twilight region of heathendom and Islam. But that does not alter the fact that the overall structure of the Middle Ages is a closed unity. God dwells in the midst of Christendom, and is to be found in the Real Presence on the altar.

The perspective of the medieval self-consciousness, however splendid it may have appeared, was none the less closed and limited. Must we not say, therefore, that the exclusiveness of the closed circle, typical of the Middle Ages, in some measure misinterprets the Christian obligation to be "catholic"?

The two forces destined to tear asunder the closed unity of the medieval world are the Reformation and the Renaissance.

Reformation and Renaissance

The general state of decadence which prevailed in the political as well as the ecclesiastical sphere during the late Middle Ages cried out for reform in every direction. A certain inflexibility in the Church—as also at the political level—was one reason why the call for a renewal of faith, when it came, caused a split in Western Christendom.

Once again Christian unity was shattered; and this brought in its train not only a geographical and quantitative constriction of the Church's universality but still further damage inflicted upon the depth-dimension of catholicity. Reaction to the process of reform gave rise to what was inevitably a one-sided emphasis on certain Christian truths—which meant that other precious aspects of Christianity were obscured. We have not sufficiently realized that in parting company with us Protestantism took a part of the Christian tradition with it, and that the total resources of the Catholic faith were impoverished as a result—how much impoverished we are only now, through our ecumenical contacts, beginning to surmise.

Without at all denying the many good aspects of the Counter-Reformation, one has to face up to the more objectionable features of this movement. What a pity it is that the Counter-Reformation originated and developed principally in those countries of Southern Europe that had no direct contact with the actual process of reform! Its religious inspiration—which was, after all, *counter*-reformational—and the forms in which that inspiration came to be expressed help to explain why from then on the Catholic Church assumed a markedly Roman or South European character. Here again there was in some sort—as we may think—a loss of catholicity.

If the Reformation gave rise to yet further division in matters of faith, the Renaissance challenged and impugned faith itself. It is not possible, of course, to describe in a few sentences such a complex phenomenon as the Renaissance; but what can be said is that in it there emerges, among other things, a particular outlook, a mentality which sees and experiences the human realm as precisely *that* and nothing else and thus has no need for God in this connection. Science and art discover man, and all that pertains to him, as an "autonomous area" which does not derive its value from the fact that it is a symbol of the divine, but is valuable and beautiful in its own right.

And so a whole chunk of "Christian world" fell away; and there came into being a new area of life, bound still to Christianity by what were at the very most certain conventional ties. At the same time the closed circle that was Europe was broken through. New worlds were discovered. "The world" was no longer identical with Christendom. New peoples and new religions popped up on the horizon. Astronomy made men familiar with the idea that the world was really no more than a tiny ball in an infinite universe. All this made a static view of the world untenable. To be alive was to be on the move—and that applied to Christianity as well. It moved, certainly; but the move was a retreat.[3]

The Modern Period

As the secularizing process is intensified in the period that now ensues, so the Church is gradually forced into a kind of private existence, outside—or at any rate alongside—the life of society. This has been described—in somewhat dramatic fashion, no doubt—as the "ghetto-izing" of the Church. On the one hand, the reason for it lies with history, which has gone in such a way as to compel her to this existence in a "religious reserve". But there was a further reason why the Church retired behind her own defences; and that was the emphasis now placed on an other-worldly piety and on the spirituality of religious experience within the Church herself.

Because of these things, the Church came to stand more and more outside the main events and movements in the world; and indeed, as often as not she adopted a hostile, or at any rate deprecatory, attitude when confronted with the political, scientific, social and industrial upheavals that from the eighteenth to the twentieth century plunged Europe into turmoil. And so when ideas of democratic freedom emerged—and burst out with explosive force in the French

Revolution—the Church remained aloof. She took a disapproving line over the development of modern science and modern thought. During the unrest that marked the social and industrial revolutions of the nineteenth century she stood for the most part on the sidelines.

All these facts—and the course things have taken—serve to show that whether we have been conscious of it or not, the task and challenge of catholicity have been understood in an ever more and more constricted way.

It has been no part of our purpose here to write history; and we must bear in mind that there is a good and positive side to those moments in history which have been singled out for comment. All that we intended was to get a bird's-eye view of the Church's history, and in so doing to reveal that, inasmuch as one thinks of catholicity as something historically realized, the picture is one of increasing restrictedness and bleakness. This is not meant to be a one-sided and destructive critique, but is simply intended to emphasize how necessary and urgent a task catholicity presents at this moment.

Quite clearly, the tendency at the Council has been towards a renewed universalism. It is important to see that the effort being made to re-establish relations with the Eastern Churches is likewise an attempt to restore catholicity—and to do so precisely in that sector where the first major loss of catholicity was suffered. Perhaps this is also the way the ecumenical movement must first set about things.

So that we can get a still better, and concrete, idea of how dangerous and destructive integralism in the Church can be, we shall now attempt a brief impression of the organized integralism that prevailed during the pontificate of Pope Pius X.

II. The Drama of Modernism

In the latter half of the nineteenth century, among a not inconsiderable number of Catholic clergy (and some lay people also—although these constituted a minority) in France, Germany, Britain, Italy and The Netherlands, there arose an earnest desire for a renewal and re-orientation of the Church. What they wished to see re-orientated was the Catholic Church's attitude towards, and rapport with, the great intellectual and spiritual movements of that time. Many argued that the Church's closed and frightened attitude was fatal to the kind of discussion so urgently needed—an open discussion of the problems of the historical method in criticism, the new critical interpretation of the Bible, the new trends of thought in philosophy and the way in which the rise of the natural sciences had made it possible to view the world from that particular standpoint. This inclination towards renewal and reform came to a head in a movement, not altogether easy to comprehend, which the church authorities themselves chose to call "modernism".

It was primarily the Frenchman, A. Loisy, who through his radical biblical criticism aimed to instil new life into the somewhat unprepossessing Catholic exegesis of Scripture. Here was an up-to-date, critical, scientific approach which had its effect on the whole field of doctrine and belief, and more especially on the area concerned with the history of dogma and of the Church. In England it was George Tyrell who spoke in favour of the primacy of religious experience, in an attempt to relativize rationalistic theology. In Germany the dogmatic theologian, Hermann Schell, assailed the superstitious element in so many popular forms of Catholic piety. His aim was an exemplary Catholicism, free from a narrow, anti-Protestant outlook.

Thus in spite of everything there were quite a number of people intensely concerned with the great issues and problems of their times. From *our* standpoint in history we are bound to say that although they perceived the questions clearly enough, in their quest for the answers these "modernists" sometimes went quite astray, or else what they proposed was enunciated in terms unacceptable to their day and age. The worst of it was, however, that ecclesiastical authority, because it was so fear-ridden, would not allow an honest attempt to resolve the great questions of the time. That is why the battle with modernism offers a painful example of a closed Catholicism, of a closed mentality that found expression first and foremost among the top circles of the hierarchy and was presumably a major consequence of the undue importance attached to papacy and curia ever since the First Vatican Council.

Pius X and modernism

The drama of modernism was played out mainly during the pontificate of Pius X (1903–1914). Not everything that happened can be laid at the door of that canonized pope. His simple origin, his aversion to the traditional, prelatical Roman diplomacy, alienated him from the college of Cardinals. That was also the reason why he came to rely more and more on a few trusted associates and thus was prejudicially and badly advised by monsignori who were wedded to integralism. The result was that Pius X ended up in isolation. In conjunction with his Secretary of State, Cardinal Merry del Val, and conscious all the time of a kind of imperative mission, he set himself in battle array against an international modernist conspiracy (largely engineered by certain clerics).

Pius X had before him in this struggle the example of his predecessor, Pius IX, who in 1864 issued an encyclical accompanied by a syllabus of eighty (explicitly censured) errors. So with the bull *Lamentabili* of 1907 Pius X drew up what was known as the "new syllabus". Some months later appeared the encyclical *Pascendi* which, as against the negative condemnatory formulas of the new syllabus, set out positively and in considerable detail the "dogma of modernism"—and again condemned it. The bull *Lamentabili* listed "the errors of the modernists" in sixty-five theses: "a medley and a fair old muddle", as Schmidlin puts it. Most of these propositions came from two books by Loisy. A smaller number were derived from the writings of Archbishop Mignot of Albi (France) and of the French historian, Albert Houtin. Later investigation has shown that the majority of these modernistic theses, so called, had been torn from their context and served up again in the crudest possible way; while in some cases sentences had been added which had the effect of upholstering the sense of what had originally been said—a tendency here, perhaps, to carry the position of the other side to the furthest possible extreme?

In the encyclical *Pascendi* we find the "system of modernism" as construed by those who compiled the encyclical itself. Since "the modernists had been so crafty" as to avoid systematizing their doctrine, it was deemed necessary to offer in this encyclical a synthesis of the various scattered heretical teachings, to reiterate them, and finally to announce the measures to be taken against this "rag-bag of all the heresies". The papal document lists a great number of dangerous "isms". It declares that, contrary to every sound doctrine of the Church, the philosophy, theology and historiography of the modernists led to agnosticism and phenomenalism, immanentism and symbolism—and thence to pantheism and atheism. The final end was the total destruction of all religion.

The countermeasures included: (1) the study of scholastic theology (especially that of St Thomas) must form the basis for any kind of theological instruction; (2) the professors at seminaries and universities must be vetted as to their scholastic principles—all who favour modernism and aim to renovate their studies of history and the Bible must be removed at once; (3) the bishops are to inhibit and confiscate any modernistic writings; (4) clergy conferences must be permitted only very occasionally; (5) in each separate diocese councils for the care and protection of the faith must be instituted; their business will be to nose out whatever may be uttered of a modernistic nature and report it immediately to Rome; (6) the bishops are to report regularly to Rome on the success, or otherwise, of these measures; and lastly, a special institute is to be set up which with the co-operation or support of all Catholic scholars will pursue the study of science in all its branches, on Catholic principles.[4]

Extreme intolerance

When one looks at these proposals, it is hard to know whether one ought to feel saddened at the totalitarian tone which marks their expression or the combination of fear and suspicion to which they testify. Of course, it all has to be set in the context of the period. One has to admit that it was the pope's job to exercise his pastoral office and to conserve the proper character of the Christian revelation and the unalterable values of the Church, in the face of certain tendencies of the time that were not without their dangers: a rationalism bent on reducing everything to a single level, and a historical relativism. But however commendable the end in view, it cannot possibly excuse the extreme intolerance and incompetence with which the matter was handled. The omnibus expression "modernism"—invented by top integralist Mgr Benigni to describe the *omnium haeresium complexus* which had been posited—was a most unhappy one, for a start. The modernist heresy—as whipped into shape by the encyclical *Pascendi*—just did not exist. Anybody could give that a wide berth. The only thing that held the eclectic document together was its violent and aggressive tone, which was attributed by some to the pope himself.

To the actual substance of the thing Pius X could certainly not have contributed a great deal. His training in philosophy, history and exegesis was hardly good enough for that; and his limited knowledge of languages (confined to Latin and Italian) did not permit him to familiarize himself with the offending literature at first hand. Who the real author of the encyclical was has remained unsettled to this very day. One of the suspects is the Spanish Capuchin Cardinal Vives y Tuto; but a Frenchman, Cardinal Billot, has been suggested too. According to the *Giornale d'Italia*, Mgr Benigni worked for a whole year on compiling *Pascendi*. Whether that is so or not, one simply cannot understand how the Roman professor, Ludwig Hertling, S. J., can say that, of its kind, the encyclical *Pascendi* is a masterpiece of theology, comparable with the Tridentine decree on justification.[5]

The most regrettable thing of all is, of course, that one of the few positive recommendations in *Pascendi*—namely, that an institute of reliable Catholic science be set up—was not implemented. The commission of Cardinals (under Cardinal Rampolla as chairman and with Freiherr Ludwig von Pastor as its secretary) which was established "for the advancement of science in the Catholic world" fell foul of various integralist machinations. Only the Higher Institute for Philosophy at Louvain (founded by Cardinal Mercier) may be regarded as perhaps a belated outcome of *Pascendi*. So as to "lay the axe to the root of the poisonous tree of modernism", three years after *Pascendi* the pope issued the *motu proprio Sacrorum antistium* (1910). This laid it down that all clergy—and especially professors at seminaries and universities—be required to take the "anti-modernist oath" once every year. Like the encyclical, this measure provoked a lot of opposition, not to say disgust. Mgr Mignot remarked arrestingly that this annual oath-taking business must inevitably lead to "mental apathy". Nowadays the oath is taken once only, that is, prior to receiving the subdiaconate. Its practical significance is slight, because usually the candidate for the superior orders is only superficially acquainted with the real object and quite specific implications lying behind the terms of the oath.

III. Integralism

Pope Pius X fancied that he had to do battle with a sort of underground modernist conspiracy that was making use of a widespread clandestine organization in order to undermine the foundations of the Catholic Church. That is why he raised no objection when a *Carbonaria* was formed—a secret society within the Church, a kind of hypercatholic freemasonry, governed by a group of men in the Roman curia. Thus the Church acquired a shadow government which, even if it did not resort to actual terrorism, was given to persistent intrigue. Among the ringleaders in this enterprise was Mgr Benigni, a short, plump and mercurial prelate, who since 1906 had been attached to the Secretariat of State. In order to carry the war on modernist heresy into every nook and cranny, however remote, he set up the secret society known as *S.P.* or *Sapinière*, that is, the *Sodalitium Pianum (the Sodality of Pius)*, which before very long had an elaborate and far-reaching organization at its disposal. Pius X, who probably did not know very much about the precise purposes of this society or the way it went to work, in 1911 and again in 1913 wrote letters in his own hand, giving it his approval and making it the responsibility of Cardinal Cajetanus de Lai, of the Consistorial Congregation.

Part of the *Sodalitium Pianum*'s machinery was an advice bureau in Rome, which received and passed on information in conditions of the utmost secrecy; and to this was added in 1912 an *Agence Internationale Roma* (AIR), for co-ordinating international contacts. Subsequently, two periodicals were started: *Borromeus*—a secret organ for journalists—and *Paulus*—a kind of intelligence bulletin, which laid down the lines of international policy and said what measures were to be taken. The integralist interest was also served by a number of weeklies, some for the chosen few and others with a wider appeal: *Rome et le monde* and *Cahiers catholiques romains*, which were associated with a large range of local publications in, for instance, Milan, Freiburg-im-Aargau, Vienna, Berlin, Cologne, Brussels, Ghent, and so on. Integralist or ultramontane weeklies or monthlies sprouted up everywhere, like so many mushrooms: *La Vigie* in France, *Die Schildwache* in Switzerland, *Rome*—under Rector Thompson's direction—in The Netherlands, the *Petrusblätter* and *Klarheit und Wahrheit* in Germany, and *Gral* in Vienna.

The ecclesiastical spy-game

President Benigni was a dab hand at espionage and played the game with considerable attention to detail. It would be funny, had the consequences not been so serious. The Monsignor's all-seeing eye earned him quite a reputation. He himself had no less than twelve aliases; and even when the pope was being referred to—or the Secretary of State—"code names" were used ("Lady Micheline" or "Michel" for the pope, and for the Secretary, "Miss Romey" or "George"). One of the confidential periodical circulars was known as *Sweet Nelly*. All this was designed to further the cause and run the modernists to ground. The noblest quarry comprised a number of bishops, priests and members of the Society of Jesus. The sitting target of this assiduous intriguing consisted partly of eminent figures in the Church; but information was laid with the pope—or rather was smuggled in to him—even against his perfectly innocuous sisters. No wonder that terror reigned in many quarters! There were not a few who no longer dared publish anything. Even an ungrounded accusation of modernism meant that the victim would be held suspect for years on end. Various priests were in this way debarred from higher office in the Church or from a university teaching career.

Pius X's successor, Pope Benedict XV, soon put an end to the integralist terror. The *Sodalitium Pianum* was abolished. Mgr Benigni found shelter with Charles Maurras' *Action Française*, a movement which Pius XI inhibited in 1921 because of its "pagan nationalism". In 1915 the entire secret records of the *S.P.*'s Brussels headquarters fell into the hands of the German High Command. They were decoded, photographed and afterwards deposited with the Roermond diocesan seminary. Had it not been for this chance discovery, our knowledge of this scandalous episode in the history of the Church would never, perhaps, have been anything like so well documented.[6]

When the question arose of beatifying Pius X, the kind of action that had been taken against the modernists constituted, at first, a major difficulty. It was asked—for example, by the Father General of the Jesuits, W. Ledochowski—whether the character of Pius X did not often evince fortitude rather than wisdom. In his address given at the beatification ceremony, Pope Pius XII made a point of stressing that Pius X had possessed the virtue of wisdom in heroic measure. This could hardly be established, however, without a thorough probe into all the documents and historical sources of information dating from the time of the conflict with modernism. When this had been carried out, it became clear that Pius X cannot be held responsible for the sometimes quite inhuman stringency with which the modernists were treated by their opponents. Even Cardinal Merry del Val was exonerated by Pius XII. Who the really guilty parties were is still far from clear; but certainly they must have been prelates, holding high position in the entourage of Pius X and acting more often than not under cover of papal authority. That a particular clique in the Vatican *can* misuse the papal authority in this way is irksome enough; and even today it can give rise to disquieting thoughts.

We have examined the ins and outs of integralism and of the modernist conflict in some detail, because—as it seems to us—we have here (and similarly in the appearing of the *Syllabus errorum* of 1864) a point where our "closed catholicism" touches bottom, as it were. Only a frank admission of the historical facts as they have just been presented will enable us to become more fully aware of the possible excesses to which misconceptions about catholicity can lead. We have to be realistic about this and understand that integralism is not dead. Far from it. There still exist in a number of countries more or less secret associations based on an integralist conception of catholicism (the expression, "more Roman than the pope", reflects an intuition which people have about this). These associations seem unduly bent on keeping things just as they are, on setting too much store by ecclesiastical authority and on putting the layman at the beck and call of the clergy. They want to subject every department of life to the *potestas directa*—the immediate control of the Church. Even now there are côteries who seem to think that their job is to winkle out progressive developments and writings wherever these appear and then lodge a complaint against them with the nunciature. In some countries the nuncios themselves are too much swayed by integralists; and they often play a somewhat ambiguous rôle in the Catholic community there as a result. This is one reason why voices have been heard at the Council, pleading for the abolition of nunciatures.

A Modernist revival?

There is a further reason why it is useful to reflect on the battle over the modernists. The present moves in the direction of renewal, re-orientation and a progressive temper generally are taken by some as evidence of a revival of modernism or as evidence of neo-modernism.[7] Since for a certain section of the hierarchy "modernism" is a concept associated very much with an extremely dangerous heresy, this is highly compromising talk and in the mouths of some people, at any rate, sounds like an accusation. But then those who are worried about a modernist revival should not forget what happened on the former occasion: the battle with the modernists meant that the dialogue—one so desperately *needed*—with contemporary modes of thought (historical criticism, the main currents of philosophy, and the outlook on the world provided by the natural sciences) was abruptly and prematurely cut short and indeed forcibly suppressed. This does not mean to say, however, that the questions and problems very properly recognized and filled out by the modernists have disappeared or have somehow taken care of themselves. They were simply pushed into the background; and now they come crowding back, thicker and faster than ever before. We cannot dodge them this time.

The frustrated theologian of the post-modernist period retreated into what was apparently safe territory—for instance, the whole area of Marian dogmas. It looked as if putting a foot wrong, doctrinally speaking, was pretty well impossible, so far as Mariology was concerned. Without wishing at all to deny the value of Marian piety and devotion, we are still bound to say that for the Catholic at odds with the world and shut up in his Catholicism it scarcely provided a way out (not to mention the chilling effect which all this had on any relationship with the Reformed). The same can be said of a zealous concentration on liturgical worship in as far as this has developed in some instances into a somewhat exclusive form of liturgical piety. However valuable to the revival of "true religion" inside the Church, it can sometimes be a cover for running away from the real problems of the Catholic, who as a Christian wants to be involved up to the neck in the life that people have to live in the world here and now—a world ridden with anxiety, and yet at the same time self-assured in its autonomy, through being at once fascinated and intimidated by the whole technical set-up into which it is more and more being drawn; a world suffering under its divisions and struggling to find its unity, but above all a world *in search* of salvation and liberation—a search that leads along many a false path, perhaps, and through ways devoid of all religious belief. Is it then for the Catholic in such a world to shut himself up in his own aesthetically proven and nicely preserved cultic forms and practices? Is he to fancy himself "already saved"—and with that hold himself discharged of all responsibility for a proclamation of the Gospel that will speak to the world of here and now, through an apprehension of its needs?

We believe that authentic catholicity demands something other than that. It demands a stance and attitude of openness; and it demands that we think and feel and suffer and search together with mankind as it is here and now in its questioning and searching and suffering.

The issues that lay concealed behind modernism have now returned in a new and more extended form. Does not true catholicity require that the Church enter into the seeking and questioning of modern man? We can only hope that this time the Church will not let or hinder these things, or try to cut them short. And because "seeking" always in some sense entails an element of "wandering here and there", we would wish to say that the Church must make a certain amount of room for that too. Her pastoral care for the ninety-and-nine ought not to mean that because of them the one lost sheep gets cut off from the flock; but like the Shepherd in the Gospel, she must go after the sheep who seeks and strays—must love it and go along with it and make it the very centre of her concern.

III

Catholicity and Non-conformism

A closed Catholicism is one which in certain respects fails to grasp what the imperative call to catholicity means. This can have dire consequences for the church community in this or that particular area, and ultimately for the Church as a whole. But it is important to remember that this fact is not always immediately appreciated. Indeed, it is possible for a church to go on for years in the belief that being closed in this way is a tremendous asset which must be hung on to at all costs. Especially when the hierarchy acts as the main champion and defender of such a position, it takes a catastrophe of some sort to bring home to the community in question just how fatal a closed Catholicism really is. The classic example of this is German Catholicism during the Hitler period. It is to be observed, so far as that goes, that even after the catastrophe a good many eyes were just as shut as they had been before it. The movement which took up the cudgels against this mental obtuseness and closed condition in the Church was referred to as non-conformism. Analysing what took place in the Catholic Church of Germany during and after the Hitler régime should give occasion for us to draw certain conclusions that may perhaps help to supply more content to the notion of catholicity.

At the end of August 1963 the German bishops met at Fulda. It was said that the episcopate had come together for joint consultation and in order to prepare for the second session of Vatican II. Between them they drew up and issued a pastoral letter which was read out in all churches on 22 September (see below, pp. 46–8). Although the letter dealt with quite a variety of subjects, only one point in it stuck in the minds of a lot of people: the censure passed on a number of non-conformists who were addicted to a false conception of the Church. It concerned—to be explicit—the writers Carl Amery (a pseudonym for Christian Mayer) and Heinrich Böll.

This latter piece of information we owe to a communiqué from the *Katholische Nachrichten Agentur* (Catholic News Agency), which was reproduced by the *K. N. P.* and subsequently prompted the appearance, in the Dutch Catholic dailies, of the following headlines: "German episcopate condemns non-conformist Catholics" *(De Tijd)*, and "Pastoral letter against modernism" *(De Volkskrant)*. If now one reads over the bishops' letter with this in mind, it becomes quite evident that no "isms" of any sort are referred to, nor is any single person mentioned by name in it. When you know that both Amery and Böll have been putting forward serious criticisms of the Church press, you may begin to suspect that we have here some very dubious and biased reporting.

All the same, the vagueness displayed by the German bishops is hardly matter for congratulation. Indeed, it is calculated to leave the way open to misuse of their text in the form of insinuations and defamatory speculation. So the big question remained: in this pastoral letter, precisely which persons are being got at? One bishop felt himself called upon to clear up the obscurity of the episcopal document. Mgr Schäufele, Bishop of Freiburg-im-Breisgau, declared in a speech that the reference was to Carl Amery and his book, *Die Kapitulation, oder deutscher Katholizismus heute*, Heinrich Böll[1] and his novel *Ansichten eines Clowns (The Clown)*, and to "numerous publications of Friedrich Heer". Of course, these are not the only people intended by the pastoral letter; for if they are the ones actually specified, others must be meant too—writers who have advanced more or less the same critical opinions. I am thinking here chiefly of Ernst Wolfgang Böckenförde, who sparked off a stormy discussion with his *Hochland* article (of February 1961), entitled: "Der deutsche Katholizismus im Jahr 1933". Then again, there are the authors who made a systematic historical study of the conduct of Catholicism in the Nazi period—men like Hans Müller, with his sober documentation in *Katholische Kirche und Nationalsozialismus* and Rudolf Hernegger in his study, *Macht ohne Auftrag, die Entstehung der Staats- und Volkskirche*. Finally, one must include the group of authors involved with the *Münchener Werkhefte*, as well as a few people who have contributed to the *Frankfurter Hefte*, such as Ida Friederike Görres and Walter Dirks.

The question why all these persons are *not* mentioned has something to do, presumably, with the fact that their writings have had no great influence or effect on the people as a whole.

A further reason for disquiet on the part of the German bishops is that criticism inside the Church runs parallel with what has been said in non-Catholic and non-German circles about the conduct of German Catholicism. It is worth mentioning in this connection a book by the American sociologist, Gordon Zahn: *German Catholics and Hitler's Wars.*[2] Zahn argues that the German bishops actually supported Hitler in his blitzkriegs. Then there came Rolf Hochhuth's play, *Der Stellvertreter (The Representative)*, the basic contention of which is that in resisting Hitler and his persecution of the Jews the Christian Churches failed, in that they sacrificed the Gospel's universal law of love to their own interests as ecclesiastical institutions. To my mind, this much discussed play is not a direct attack on Pius XII; but it does make him a symbol of the way the Churches behaved.

If now, in the light of what has just been said, we ask who—*in fact* and practically speaking—were being got at in the bishops' letter, we are left with two names that really stand up: those of Heinrich Böll and Carl Amery; for these two writers have given us their ideas in novels or in the form of an extremely engaging prose polemic, and as a result, they have had a very considerable influence on wide sections of the public—an influence still further enhanced when on several occasions their published work was used as a springboard for discussion on radio and television and was made the subject of several fiercely controversial articles in the daily press. Heinrich Böll has pilloried the rigid institutionalism, the closed mentality and conformism within the Church, not only in his book *The Clown* but also in his papers, *Brief an einen jungen Katholiken, Polemik eines Verärgerten,* and above all in his *Nachwort* or epilogue to Amery's book, where without any reservations he takes his stand with Amery on the latter's principal arguments.

To my mind, it is Amery in particular who sums up with most sharpness, clarity and depth of insight—and with the least ceremony—what has to be said about German Catholicism in its concrete aspects (its structures, pronouncements and ideas). In a word, what his critique tilts at is the *closed catholic mentality*; and by this is meant not simply that the Church's attitude towards other groups and currents of opinion is a closed one, but that the Church exhibits the "closed ranks" character of a military formation (cf. the passage in the song *Die Reihen fest geschlossen*), in which the individual gets swallowed up in an undifferentiated, closed conformity. This tightly knit, insalubrious conformism in German Catholic life is not to be gainsaid; and the opposition to it is quite accurately described, therefore, as a *non-conformism*.

Amery's protest

Amery's basic argument could be expressed in these terms: in its thinking, its value-judgments, its religious stance, its moral ethos and its structures of command German Catholicism does not permit itself to be governed first and foremost by a steady confrontation with the Gospel, but is broadly determined by the ideas, ethics and received structures taken for gospel in the *petit-bourgeois*, provincial sector of society. Amery goes on, by employing a technique of historical and sociological analysis, to show that this is indeed the true state of affairs. He means to say that the part of society from which Catholicism draws its real support—that is, the "citizen-farmer" confraternity as a social unit—has its own creed and code of morals and is prepared to back these, as a sort of pseudo-religion, against the real stuff of Christianity. It is important, therefore, at this point, to try and get clear what, broadly speaking, the content of this quasi-faith and this quasi-morality is.

What might be called the "credal content" of this environmentally conditioned Catholicism is for a large part defined by what people conceive "Church" to be. Despite the better insight at a high level, the ordinary run of Church life is still based, in practice, on a view of the Church that derives from the nineteenth century. One might put it like this: the Church is first and foremost an educational institution, a carefully guarded *stockade*, a spiritual nature-reserve, within which the faithful are guided and governed by solicitous overseers whose job is to prescribe the rules, rubrics and regulations and to hand out directives. The sum total of these rules, precepts and directives is, for the majority, *the* Christian, churchly life. Not *what* people are, not *that* they are the Church—these things have no part in the idea of what it means to belong to the Church; but whether one toes the line, and for whom, and in what respects—this is what really matters. Hence whenever anybody chooses to repudiate some precept, usage or rule—even if it has become quite pointless in itself—this is regarded as disobedience and as breaking with a sacred tradition.

Such a notion of the Church is in close accord with the values that predominate in the setting of German rural provincialism; and that no doubt explains why this "picture" of the Church has survived for so long. In the world of this Catholicism, with its special setting, clerical authority is the overriding factor which ensures by every accepted means of custom and office that in all they think and do the sheep stay within the fold. Should a wolf approach the flock, the sheep are not expected to turn themselves into bloodhounds. The rough stuff is left to the powers that be which, after all, are there for that very purpose. If the sheep make any showing at all, it is by their closed and conformist demeanour within the fold.[3]

When we enquire what this "creed" involves in practice, in terms of actual living, the decisive factor would appear to be the absence of controversy of any kind; for Catholicism is a homogeneous "thing"—any admission of difference or variation, however slight—let alone any show of resistance to obsolete structures—is of the devil and therefore thoroughly damnable. The whole set-up absolutizes *its* Catholicism and presents it as the one and only genuine article. The ecclesiastical line is to turn inwards, stay put, and venerate the *status quo*.

So far as the *mores*, the ethics, of this particular milieu are concerned, everything centres on a system or scheme of meritorious qualities, the greatest of these being the civic virtue of decorum or respectability *(Anstand)*. This *Anstand, Anständigkeit*, is the sum of all the virtues accepted and acclaimed in such a society. They include honesty, unflagging industry, prompt and regular springing to the call of one's duty and service, a mistrust of whatever is out of the usual run and likely, therefore, to have an unsettling effect—such as the impulse to get things renewed or changed, or the urge to have done with outworn traditions. But we have not yet got to the most important virtue of all: *a submissiveness and readiness to knuckle under*, which it is right and proper to show towards the powers that be. Amery remarks that what we have here are certain second-order qualities and that the primary Christian virtues of faith, hope and charity, of humility and of "sitting loose" to the things of this world, if they are not entirely absent from this code of respectability, are certainly not of capital importance in it.

Amery's conclusion is that the flat identification of this conditioned Catholicism with Catholicism *tout simple* constitutes a serious threat to the fulfilment of the Church's commission in the world. The stranglehold which environmental factors have over German Catholicism means that it is in no position to work out a Christian ethics or to present Christianity in such a way that it will make sense and attract people powerfully to the faith. The conception of the Church and the whole system of faith and morals are such that they have become a grave hindrance to the credibility of the message proclaimed and to the concrete presence of the Church in the world of today. The result is that a Christian existence—the real thing—is distorted, if it is not destroyed.

With himself and other non-conformists in mind, Amery goes on to say that anybody who rebels against the environment and the system is branded as a falsifier of Christianity and hounded out as no better than an enemy.

Thus Amery—and with him Heinrich Böll—concludes that when German Catholicism during the Nazi period was faced with the demands of Christianity in a radical form, this type of conditioned Catholicism capitulated. It is certain that German Catholicism, at least up to 1939, did not lift a finger for liberty, or for the Jews, or for the victims of the concentration camps. People just hoped that so long as the Church could hold Catholics together *as a self-contained group*, the worst could somehow be avoided, perhaps even that through a measure of loyalty to the régime the good old order of things might be reinstated.

The drama of 1933

For most of the non-conformists, the point at which the unhealthy character of this Catholicism and its closed position within its environment became acutely obvious is the take-over of power in 1933. It simply was not equipped to offer any really effective resistance. The whole mechanism of the set-up put any such possibility out of court—I mean, its vulnerability, its dependence on directives and authorities, its suspicion of large historical initiatives and its instinctive notion of Christian existence as a bundle of precepts and "moral standards".

The bulk of the Catholic part of the nation adopted a "wait and see" attitude, little suspecting then how poorly equipped it was for the coming struggle and failing to realize that the strategy at its command was hopelessly outmoded. For one of the major difficulties was that German Catholicism was so beautifully organized in a political party, in every conceivable kind of professional association and youth movement. This complex of organizations, spreading out in so many directions, dated from the time of the *Kulturkampf*; and this *Kampf*, which had been fought out on issues relating to the *Kulturpolitik* (i.e., questions of the relationship between Church and State), had on the whole proved to be not a bad thing for religious freedom. In the past, this "organizational" way of going about things had shown that it could get things done; and at that time it made possible an effective campaign *with the apparatus and techniques of the closed mentality*: namely, the use of the mass vote, resolutions by this or that organization and manifestoes in the press. But for the battle-fields of 1933 the organization-system was totally inadequate, was indeed a fatal weakness. The new State under Hitler employed precisely the *Kulturkampf* technique—but turned it round the other way. Hitler made the old *Kulturpolitik* dream of a concordat with the State come true; but by means of the so-called "equalization" policy he ensured the complete powerlessness of the organizations—which he allowed to continue, admittedly, so long as he could exploit them as instruments of this policy.

The rôle of the Centre Party was ended by the "Plenary Powers' Act", as it was called; and the Party did Hitler the favour of liquidating itself. But Catholic organizations, *Gesellenvereine* (Fellowships) and youth movements continued until late in 1934 to join in declarations of loyalty and in acclaiming the Führer, till they too were thrown on the scrapheap. The big question is: how did the episcopate and the Catholic organizations come to make a declaration of loyalty so soon after Hitler's seizure of power?

Some interesting documents have since come to light, which bear on this question. On 25 March 1933, two days after Hitler's governmental declaration, which promised that the interests of *Kulturpolitik* (the very issues on which the *Kulturkampf* had been waged) would be safeguarded. Cardinal Bertram of Breslau wrote to the Fulda and Bavarian Bishops' Conference to put to the episcopate a two-fold proposal for a declaration of loyalty. He asked for a "yes or no" reply by telegram, because—he said—there was not much time to lose. To justify this, he added the following observations:

> 1. To wait and see whether the government will implement all the splendid promises contained in the Reich-Chancellor's basic policy statement will mean that it must be years before any clear and definite position is reached. Nothing could be worse than that. I would think it right, therefore, for us to take advantage of this moment to go as far as our faith and the law of the Church permit.
>
> 2. In the major Catholic cities, where at the moment the S.S. are not admitted in close formation to Catholic services, attendance at church services is part of standing orders. The result is that Catholic members of the S.S. proceed in close column to the Protestant church. This will happen more and more . . .

Thus the Cardinal. This brief passage puts quite plainly and openly what the Catholic leaders were after: (1) a clear agreement between State and Church, and (2) the preservation of a self-contained Catholicism. Encouraged by the bishops' declaration of loyalty and still more by the insistent ploys of Mgr Kaas (a prelate attached to the Centre Party) and of the crafty Catholic politician, Von Papen, the Vatican concluded that there were no cogent reasons why a concordat should not be signed. And so, on 30 July 1933—scarcely four months after the take-over of power—this agreement between Hitler-Germany and the Vatican came into being.

Heinrich Böll was later to write regarding this episode that one of the biggest moral hazards of his younger days was the circumstance that the Vatican had been the first State to conclude a treaty with Hitler. He recalls, with much bitterness, that after the ratification of this treaty it was very much the done thing to go to the communion rail in S.S. uniform. As soon as Mass was over and one was back on duty, one could sing without a single qualm: *Wenn das Judenblut vom Messer spritzt. . . .* ("When Jewish blood spurts from the knife . . .").[4]

What came of the pledge of allegiance and the concordat, we know. But still, what was in the minds of the German bishops at that time? Let us not forget: "self-containment" was the great Catholic achievement of the nineteenth century. So long as the Church were able to keep things that way—or so it was thought—it would be safe, as it had been in the *Kulturkampf*, to rely on the external arm of the pledge of loyalty, and the internal arm of its own self-containment, to strike down the old enemies—the old enemies who were to be feared more than Nazism itself: liberalism, socialism and "immorality in general". Then again, Hitler's anti-communism provided the Catholic leaders with a kind of absolution for having collaborated with the régime. They liked to think that Hitler was a vehicle chosen by Providence to slay the dragon of bolshevism. The final victory over communism seemed more important than the fate of six million Jews. . . Perhaps the good old days could even be restored. People thought: what was good enough for the *Kulturkampf* is good enough to stand up to National Socialism. But alas! what were the tactics of yesterday may spell nothing but disaster for tomorrow and today. "Self-containment" is not in itself a value—certainly not an essentially Christian one. In the struggle with the Nazis such tactics were not only senseless; they were highly dangerous.

In the years that followed people clung to the *idée fixe*

of "self-containment", in spite of the very indifferent experience they had had with it in the first months after the Nazis' accession to power. As we have already said, the whole organization-system capitulated promptly and without a murmur. But even later on, when nothing remained to be seen but the ranks of the Party itself, *still* nothing changed; and "self-containment" was still the tactical order of the day. People went just "as far as the faith and the law of the Church permit"; that is, they withdrew behind the inner bastion of the terms of the concordat, and went on hoping that somehow the good old days would return.[5]

Further capitulation

Amery goes on to survey Catholic strategy between the years 1935 and 1945. What it amounts to is that the concordat was adhered to with typical German punctiliousness, despite Hitler's trampling all over the agreement with complete savagery. Every time a breach of the concordat was perpetrated, all the Church did was to remind the government of its promises and obligations. The nature and extent of Catholic resistance were laid down by the episcopate, which took upon itself the whole burden of initiative—as is evident from a pastoral letter of Cardinal Von Galen's (1933). In this situation the Catholic people were called upon to display the good old virtues of the bourgeois code and tradition: obedience to ecclesiastical and secular authority, a policy of "sticking close together", and avoidance of anything like insurrectionist behaviour or activities *(umstürzlerischen Verhalten)*, as the closing passage of the *Fuldauer Erklärung* (Declaration) of March 1933 puts it. The resistance offered by individuals or by small groups, not being sanctioned by the episcopate, was therefore not only disowned but rejected and actively opposed.

Happily, however, such tactics did not mean that resistance was entirely lacking in Catholic circles. There were those who paid the penalty—but these were only individual victims, who got no support either from the episcopate or from those around them. So when they now put up in Berlin a pretentious concrete church with the name of *Regina Martyrum* and tell us that this is in honour of the great Catholic leaders of the Resistance, there is an element of gross hypocrisy and disrespect for truth here somewhere; because that resistance never got any backing from the Catholic sector at large. A more suitable name for this church, one would have thought, would be *Mea Culpa*.

Remorselessly, one might say, Amery pursues his historical analysis still further. He points out that the Catholic military pastorate simply prevaricated over the major issues of conscience which troubled so many soldiers, and that it was the unforthcoming attitude of the Catholics that stymied efforts to solve the refugee problem after the war. The monetary annulment of 1948, which marked the beginning of the *Wirtschaftswunder* (the "miracle" of German economic recovery), brought no change in the Catholic system of approved values—or approved virtues, for that matter. The old spirit of self-containment showed itself once more in the close line-up between the Church and the C.D.U. (Christian Democratic Union)—an alliance that came to be not far short of identification. Böll speaks, with biting sarcasm, of a new trinity: Frings, Adenauer and the *Rheinische Merkur* (i.e., the paper, *The Rhineland Mercury*). In Amery's view, the only hope for German Catholicism is to detach the Church from just the one political party, to find a place within the Church for healthy controversy, persuade her to be open to justifiable criticism and to admit her share of responsibility for the past—but above all to recreate the whole image of the Church in terms of the liturgical movement: the Church is first and foremost the "congregation of Christ", and not a closed milieu, dominated by its characteristic code. Catholics must be treated as adults and must learn to search their own consciences and not fall back on a collective conscience moulded by episcopal ordinaries and their pronouncements.

We do not have to agree with everything that Amery and

Böll say. Their criticism is frequently much too sharp and angry and embittered. Although that is easy to understand, and although this kind of criticism is always bound to be rather fierce and intemperate, the feelings of these writers have run away with them. There are a lot of pretty hasty generalizations, things are sometimes oversimplified by being painted too much in black and white, there are gaps and inaccuracies in the historical documentation, and their conclusions often go too far. And then these writers do not seem to have taken any account of the bishops, priests and lay people who have always made a stand against the ideas and outlook of the milieu. They pass over too easily the positive assets of German Catholicism (which includes the positive German contribution to the Council), which it is difficult to explain in terms of a sectionally conditioned Catholicism.

Yet Amery's fundamental thesis cannot be swept aside: Catholicism in Germany is dominated in its structures, tactics, behaviour and outlook by the values and ideas of one particular social sector, the petit-bourgeois, rustic milieu. In the situation of major crisis created by National Socialism German Catholicism failed, therefore, to match up to the basic requirements of Christianity.

The non-conformists and the hierarchy

What the non-conformists hoped for more than anything else was that their writings would spark off a fruitful discussion about the new direction that German Catholicism ought to take. They expected that the episcopate too would play a stimulating and guiding rôle in it. This hope and expectation have received a nasty jolt, however, especially from the contents of the pastoral letter of 22 September 1963. So as to make the contrasting positions clear, I propose to allow myself a somewhat lengthier quotation from the document in question:

> ... We turn our anxious attention to the false ideas regarding the Church which have been getting about here and there

among Catholics, and especially among intellectuals. There is a good deal of criticism being expressed of the Church and of her past and present conduct. This is not just criticism of the sinfulness and human limitations of the "Church *en route*", but springs from a perverted and frequently even heretical conception of the Church as such. These critics construct an ideal picture of the Church, wholly at odds with the real situation—as though the Church consisted only of such people as are entirely filled with a charismatic spirit. There are many for whom a "Church of martyrs" is their private, but of course highly one-sided, exemplar. They regard every creative encounter of the Church with culture and society at various periods of history as a defection from an allegedly pure and primal pattern.

The fundamental mystery of the Church, however, is the mystery of the Incarnation; and that is why, at any given time, she is bound to disclose herself in the forms and patterns of culture and human society. This means too that the Church will always consist of saints and sinners, of a few prophetic figures and a large number of ordinary, run-of-the-mill people among her membership. During this period of the Council, there is one thing that we must keep sight of: all attempts on the part of your bishops to speak up for a vital concept and doctrine of the Church, for a mode of life for the Church that will be fruitful and relevant to the present time, for the peculiar responsibility that the Catholic laity have towards the world—all these efforts will immediately become problematical in the eyes of the other conciliar Fathers, so long as at the same time German Catholics keep throwing down the gauntlet with quibbles and qualifications which are in any case based on a privately fabricated and faulty interpretation of revelation and of the Church's history. These then are further reasons why this mistaken attitude fills us with concern.

Of course there is a need at this juncture for German Catholics—and especially young people—to inform themselves and increasingly to discuss these things; but then the discussion and the information must proceed from a sense of responsibility and loyalty and love for the Church. Condemnatory pronouncements by the magisterium and warnings and exhortations on the part of the bishops are not enough. It is for every one of you, according to his ability, his influence and his position at the moment, to answer the call.

The immediate impression one gets from this letter is of a somewhat authoritarian father addressing—more in sorrow than in anger—his erring children. So far as I can see, the bishops have not read their Amery very well; and they do not give much evidence of understanding the real problems that the non-conformists have posed. They would appear to be in favour of talking things out; but in point of fact they reject any such course of action by taxing the authors who are on the carpet with irresponsibility and with failing to have any faith in, or love for, the Church. It is all too easy to hook the supposed criticism on to an allegedly "false way of thinking about the Church". The debate about the course of German Catholicism is guillotined with (covertly authoritarian) threats of "condemnation" and by sticking a label marked "heretic" on to the offenders. Indeed, the people are enjoined, as it were, to form part of a sort of general inquisition, since episcopal admonitions and cautionings do not seem to help. What this inquisition is supposed to do, however, remains far from clear; and what is pointed to as false doctrine finds no sanction in anything that the non-conformists are contending.

For in fact the so-called "false picture" of the Church is not to be found in any of the non-conformist writers. Neither Amery nor Böll in fact holds that the Church "consists only of such people as are entirely filled with a charismatic spirit". For none of these writers, in fact, is a "Church of martyrs" the arcane model or examplar for the Church in every age. Moreover, they do not regard every creative encounter of the Church with culture and human society as a "defection from a pure and primal pattern". I have been unable to discover this phrase, "pure and primal pattern"—or anything like it—in either Böll or Amery. Amery's critical standpoint is based precisely on his opposition to this idea of a "real" (i.e., "spiritualized") Church.

Admittedly, he does employ the expression "Church of the martyrs"; but how is one to deny that in times of persecution the Church is called to be a martyr-church? Amery does not see this as the ideal pattern, as the way the Church should always be. He thinks precisely as the bishops do when they plead the incarnation and the fact of human frailty: he thinks *incarnationally*, that is, in terms of sociology and history. He reckons with a Church of sinners and saints—a Church whose task it is, down the ages of history, to offer an inspired response to concrete social and historical structures, from the standpoint of the Gospel. He reckons with a human Church, which in the response it offers is and always will be very human indeed. In the end, what Amery and Böll are concerned with is a critique related to what one might, roughly speaking, describe as "structures". They see that there are no good structures—none "good once and for all", that is—but that there are particular historical situations, and that the Church can respond to these with structures good, bad or indifferent. They reckon with a Church that can err in the response it makes.

It is discouraging, therefore, to find that the bishops—at any rate so far as their pastoral letter goes—display so little understanding of this current of non-conformism and so little readiness to engage in open discussion.[6]

The significance of non-conformism

We intend now to try and dig a little deeper into certain aspects of what non-conformism implies, both for the Church in Germany and for the whole of Western Catholicism.

1. German Catholicism during the Nazi period is obviously a classic example of a kind of ambiguity in Catholicism itself—something that the French philosopher, M. Merleau-Ponty, has characterized as a fundamental trait peculiar to Catholicism. The Catholic, he says, is a person who oscillates between incarnation and transcendence. In so far as the Catholic thinks along the lines of incarnation, history may

be said to advance—and the Christian may be a revolutionary. But recognition of the eternal, transcendent realm of the Father makes the Christian a conservative. Now this means that the Catholic can really only "fall in" with a revolution that has already succeeded; but he cannot himself make a revolution. Revolution always means revolt against the existing order, in so far as this fails to give proper satisfaction. The Catholic, *qua* Catholic, will have no feeling for the future; only when the future has become the "here and now" can he really make it his own. It is the way things are that reflects the will of the transcendent God.

Now there are things to be said against this view of the matter, no doubt; but the question is whether Catholicism *in fact*—as a matter of experience—does not often work out this way: the existential phenomenologist takes his cue, surely, from the actual situation. Merleau-Ponty sees revolution or total revolt as an event in which the inner dynamic of history unfolds. But because the Catholic believes in a transcendent God—that is to say, a God above and beyond history—he finds it difficult to commit himself heart and soul to the inner dynamic of history. There is one circumstance, however—so Merleau-Ponty argues—in which the Church advises and commends insurgence; and that is when an established régime violates the law of God. But in fact it has never been known for the Church to rebel against lawfully established authority for this reason. It has, of course, been known for the Church to extend her support to insurgents because they were protecting her sacred buildings, her ministers, her property. God enters fully into history, however, only when the Church feels that her duty is as much *towards all men* as to her ministers; when she feels as much concern for the houses of a city in danger as for her own temples. Thus there is such a thing as Christian insurgence—but it is qualified: it only comes into play when the Church is herself threatened.[7]

German Catholicism reacted against National Socialism,

not because it constituted a threat to humanity but because it threatened the German Catholic Church (with some emphasis here on her outward aspect and structures). It was thought at first that a compromise might settle the business. People were prepared to overlook the depravity inherent in Nazism, its brutal methods and infamous policies, provided the régime would leave the Church alone. Not until the Church in Germany was itself in danger did we get the fiery protest embodied in *Mit brennender Sorge* (1937), an encyclical in which National Socialism was not mentioned in so many words, but in which it was—even if in guarded terms and in a fairly roundabout way—none the less condemned. It talks about the Church as defender of natural law; but it is evident that in this ecclesiastical document the Church is not in the first place contending for the preservation of elementary human rights, but for her own right to existence. It still declares at the end of the encyclical that the pope has no dearer wish than that "true peace between Church and State in Germany might be restored. If however —through no fault of ours—such a peace is not to be, then the Church of God will come to the defence of her rights and liberties."[8]

The way in which the Church behaved during the period of National Socialist ascendancy at all events raises a serious question—a question not unrelated to marxist thinking on Christianity: is the ambiguous character of the tension between incarnation and transcendence an essential feature of the Church's Christianity? And if we want to answer that it is not, what are the nature and source of our confusion with regard to what Catholicism lays upon us?

2. *The* great aim that the non-conformists have set themselves is *die Bewältigung der Vergangenheit*, or as we might say: "laying the ghost of the past". The biggest thorn in the flesh consists not so much in the fact that German Catholicism of the recent past failed to come up to scratch, but that *now* the fact is still not being admitted. The past is shrugged off; or else the dark pages of the story are removed from

the book, and the pretence is maintained that "we didn't do so badly in the Hitler period, after all". It is with this in view that those booklets are put about with stories of the great leaders of the Catholic "Resistance".

Böll and Amery are making the point—fairly enough, it seems to me—that in the Catholic house beautiful of today one really must not behave as though there were no skeleton in the cupboard. The past is being hailed far too much in a spirit of *self-exoneration*; and that is something which the Catholics generally share with a lot of Germans. When visiting Germany I have questioned a number of distinguished people about the darker aspects of the past; and it has struck me how often, by way of self-absolution, they have given me the stock reply: "Ah, well, the Nazis did that!" Would it be such a terrible thing for the Catholic Church in Germany to be honest and admit to a measure of complicity (which after all was perhaps more a sin of omission—a responsibility by default—than anything else)? Not until that responsibility has been squarely shouldered will it be possible to bring into the open the major errors of past history. Only then shall we be in a position to draw from past mistakes a lesson profitable for today.

3. The "closed shop" policy of German Catholicism—its unforthcoming attitude and spirit of self-containment—has proved to be one of the fundamental mistakes of the past. The danger threatens once again—and this time because of the close alliance of the episcopate with the central organ of the whole organization complex (The Central Committee of German Catholics) and with the party structure of the C.D.U. What is so dangerous is the idea that everything tending to fortify this alliance is good, while whatever unsettles and undermines it must be wrong. The "Central Committee", which embraces a great part of the Church press, is the self-styled representative of all twenty-six million German Catholics. It in fact sets itself up as a mouthpiece of the episcopate and the Catholic sector within the German nation. This, of course, is one more expression of

the traditional, environmentally conditioned and closed "ghetto mentality"; and it is most disquieting.

What has to come now—and it is an urgent necessity—is some recognition of the real state of affairs: that there are other Catholics and Catholic groupings unable to identify themselves with either the "Central Committee" or the C.D.U. People must open their minds, in other words, to the fact that all Catholics do not think or feel in the same way about everything, that there are distinctions to be drawn and that differences—different levels of experience—among Catholics are normal and right. There must be room—room even for non-conformists. People must learn to have done for good and all with the collective anxiety-neurosis which gives rise to forced attitudes and to those spasmodic outbursts of self-justification regarding the past and to the embattled, barrack-room atmosphere that even now continues to prevail.

4. For Catholicism here in the West the recent history of the Catholic Church in Germany should be a solemn warning. Ever since the Counter-Reformation, "showing a solid front to the outsider" and a "no concessions at any price" policy has passed for *the* great Catholic virtue. The extremes to which this can lead are very clearly demonstrated in the crisis that German Catholicism was obliged to undergo. If there is talk nowadays of a crisis for Western Christianity, one of the reasons for it could well be the fact that in many Western countries the Church has come to be identified with one particular class, régime or pattern of culture. The Church's business is to be incarnated in the culture of each and every time and place. That is an essential task which her catholicity lays upon her. But incarnation must never be allowed to become total identification.

During and after the Middle Ages, the Church was too much identified with feudalism and the European supranationalism of the Holy Roman Empire. That is why the rise of nationalism could mean a break with the Church; and that is in fact what happened with the Reformation. The earliest attempts to evangelize China failed because the Church had identified herself too closely with Western forms of Christianity and Christian experience. Before and after the French Revolution it became apparent that the Church had been all too fervently attached first to the *ancien régime* and afterwards to the bourgeois milieu. The Church in the West has not succeeded, either, in creating a specifically Catholic *modus vivendi* for the industrial worker. The only effort in this direction that seemed to give any promise of success—the priest–worker movement in France—fell foul of the integralist opposition.

A closed Catholicism such as has once more reared its head in Germany points to an absence of real "catholicity", and especially of its incarnational aspect. A certain tendency to identify exclusively with a particular class or sectional interest is a danger always with us.

5. The German bishops' reaction to non-conformism is one more indication of how little understanding the hierarchy would appear to have, when it comes to the emergence of new structures within the Church. For years now they have been going on about "a lay apostolate", the "priesthood of all believers", "Catholic Action" and "the place of the layman in the Church". In spite of all the theorizing about this, very little has so far been done in practice to settle the question of *what actually are the layman's peculiar place and function in the Church*. Wits have been known to describe Catholic Action as "organized interference by the clergy with the apostolic mission of the laity". In point of fact, the layman is still treated far too much as a target for pastoral care exercised by clergymen. He is one of that passive flock, "the church people", and is required to follow submissively the line laid down by the clerics. This sort of attitude reflects a nineteenth-century conception of the Church, the disastrous effects of which we have seen working themselves out in German Catholicism.

The German episcopate is full of fine talk about "the peculiar responsibility of the Catholic laity for the world" *(die Eigenständigkeit der Weltverantwortung des Katholischen Laien)*; but there is precious little practical implementation of this particular responsibility so far as one can see. What is evident is a measure of anxiety at the enfranchisement of the layman—an enfranchisement which is now, little by little, growing and struggling towards some sort of realization. An increasing number of Catholic lay people nowadays are so well informed theologically that they can take on the clergy and converse with them on equal terms. By this I do not wish to imply that it is only Catholic intellectuals who are entitled or equipped to play an adult rôle in the Church's affairs. I simply want to make the point that those who hold office in the Church are in real danger of regarding themselves as in *sole* possession of these gifts of mind and spirit.

Granted, of course—and I am not contesting it—that the layman owes obedience to the hierarchy and to all those who by virtue of their office are charged with the task of government and proclamation in the Church; but that is only *one* side of the clergy–laity relationship. For *the hierarchy, the clergy, must also obey the layman.* If this latter remark causes some astonishment, that is because we have taken a too exclusive view—especially since the Counter-Reformation—of what "obeying" or "obedience" means, understanding it as "a subjection of the will" (that is to say, obedience to, or compliance with, a closed, conformist outlook and line of conduct). But the word and the idea of "obedience" come from the Latin: *obedire* = *ob-audire*. The basic meaning, in other words, is "hearing", in the sense of "listening to" and "being open to" something or somebody. It expresses an open and receptive state of readiness to understand, and to respond to the demands or challenge of, the other party. And that is what I mean when I say that the hierarchy must obey the layman.

Christianity—especially in its ecclesial character—can easily become rigid, imbued wth respectable, middle-class principles and mentally undernourished. To get us out of this sort of spiritual cul-de-sac, from time to time the Spirit of God raises up *prophets*, whose task and vocation it is to rouse mankind, Christendom, the Church, out of a mental and spiritual lethargy. The prophet was always turning up among the people of Israel and in the Church of former times. If we in our day no longer hear much talk of prophets, could that perhaps not be because the clerical sector of the Church claims to have an exclusive right over all prophetic activity and charismata? So far as the more recent past is concerned, perhaps the voice of prophecy, when it happened to come from the laity, has all too often been nipped in the bud.

It is worth putting on record in this connection that, vexed though they may be at the over-institutionalized churchianity of the sectional, bourgeois interest, this has not driven Böll, Amery and the rest out of the Church (as was wont to happen not at all infrequently in the 'thirties). This points to a truly Christian solicitude about the Church; and we may well wonder whether we are not compelled to detect in what they have to say a prophetic voice that demands to be understood. "What is at stake here is the Church," Amery has declared, "and were it not so, there would be absolutely no reason for writing this book".

The Church—and the hierarchical Church in particular—must always be open to all wisdom which, although it may have come "up from below", may still perhaps have been inspired by the Spirit. She must discern the new but proper and distinctive place of the layman in the Church (the structure of which, if only in vague outline, is now beginning to appear) and must make room for it. But of this we shall be hearing more in the next chapter.

I am firmly convinced myself that at this juncture an open Catholicism is vitally necessary to the further existence of the Church. In what will this "openness" consist? It means this: that enough free room will have to be created to make possible a healthy controversy and a salutary dialectic between the different groups, tendencies and environments. It means too being open towards a condition of pluriformity within the Church, in the consciousness that uniformity and conformism are the chief impediments to fruitful dialogue with everybody else.

IV

Catholicity inside the Church

I. Civil Rights for the Theologian

In this and the following chapter we intend to try and take a good look at what "catholicity" ought to signify inside the Church. By "catholicity inside the Church" we mean the openness which must prevail there on the question of expounding and justifying the faith. That is to say, it is not for one group within the Church to set itself apart and then claim an absolute and exclusive right to say what is what in theology and to formulate it correctly. One has the impression that a particular group in the higher ranks of the ecclesiastical hierarchy have in fact taken it upon themselves to exercise the magisterium in just such a way. Far be it from us to cast doubt on the teaching authority in the Church or to undermine its rightful claim to existence. But the question is: how ought this authority to be *understood?* And then we sometimes get the impression that through some kind of notion that they participate in papal infallibility the theologians in the Holy Office, for example, think that *their* theology has got to be the basis and criterion for theological enquiry throughout the whole Church. Now we do not wish to deny the value of "Roman theology"—quite the contrary; but the principle of catholicity implies that other theologies too have a right to exist within the Church, and that theologians who so far as in them lies are responsible people ought not to be deprived of the right to *a free expression of their opinions*.

We will not go all that far back into history; but we do want to recall that Teilhard de Chardin, for instance, was forbidden to publish any philosophical or theological works during his lifetime. It was not so very long ago, either, that a temporary silence was imposed on four of France's best theologians, Henri de Lubac, Yves Congar, M. D. Chenu and Jean Daniélou; and they were forced to lay all their writings before the Holy Office for special examination. In 1962 the Austrian theologian, Karl Rahner, had to submit to special censorship everything that he wrote as well (although this requirement has since been withdrawn). Rahner again is one of today's best theologians. On 25 May 1963—when Pope John lay dying—the Sacred Congregation for Seminaries and Universities issued an instruction requiring Catholic universities to obtain permission from Rome whenever they wish to confer an honorary degree. The issuing of this instruction was connected with the fact that the Catholic university of St Louis, in the U.S.A., had conferred an honorary doctorate on the youthful but highly promising theologian and *peritus* at the Council, Hans Küng. Serious efforts have been set afoot to gag this theologian too, and to deny him liberty to publish. The Catholic university of Nijmegen was perhaps the instruction's earliest victim: an interdict arrived from Rome, forbidding the university to confer an honorary doctorate on an *Anglican* scholar.

These and suchlike measures made sense, perhaps, in other times; but to the minds of many Catholics they have ceased to be compatible with the spirit of openness and renewal which is abroad today. The right to engage in "open" discussion must surely belong to the basic minimum of "civil rights" within the Catholic Church.

It goes against all true catholicity when a particular sector of the Church claims sole possession of "catholic truth" and then, without due examination or any consultation or discussion, uses the institutional apparatus at its disposal to smother at birth every dissident opinion. The outcome is a state of bondage and of anxiety and frustration on the part of many theologians. In order to put a stop to this sort of thing, Pope Paul VI, at the start of the second session of the Council, announced a drastic revision and reorganization of the Roman Curia. The moment was well chosen. For during the first session the enthusiasm for renewal shown by many of the Council Fathers had been tempered by the discovery that various important initiatives of Pope John or of the Council itself were not getting off the ground or hardly so —because a massive and intractable Roman administrative machine was at work behind the scenes, thwarting and obstructing them. Those who ventured to criticize this Roman Curia—as has appeared quite evident in The Netherlands—ran the risk of being censured, or of a monition, or of something that looked very much like proscription. The tactics of the Holy Office were a source of perpetual annoyance; and Cardinal Ottaviani and his secretary, Fr Tromp S.J., came to symbolize, pretty well in person, a totalitarian ecclesiastical power and a retrogressive movement in the highest circles of government within the Church.

Not only were lots of ecumenical Catholics embarrassed in front of their friends in the Reformed Churches, but many a Catholic felt himself discredited, as a Catholic, at the bar of international opinion. When the personality of Pope John won the hearts of Christians and non-Christians alike, and when the Council afterwards came under the spotlight of worldwide publicity, interest in the Catholic Church reached global proportions. And so the tactics of the Roman Curia were no longer simply an affair of private concern to the Church but were continually being put to the test of world opinion. Now it may be said that where matters of faith are concerned we have no business bothering our heads about world opinion. But this had nothing to do with matters of faith: it was a question of a course of action or conduct deemed to be in conflict with an elementary freedom of the human person.

It is sometimes said that the attacks on the Holy Office and on, for example, Cardinal Ottaviani have been too sharp. That is true enough. The reaction against certain highly placed ecclesiastical figures would seem to me unwarranted and unfair, if what is intended is to turn them—and with them all the so-called "conservatives"—out of the positions of influence in the Church and to silence their voices altogether. It would be downright injustice, it seems to me, to seek to eliminate the "conservative" element. The conservatively-minded element has a not unimportant place in the Church—if it be only to act as a brake on the more fanatical renovators and to keep them somewhat within bounds. As it is, however, the conservative element has got the upper hand to such an extent that any other voice is scarcely able —or permitted—to make itself heard. Only the presence of a body of bishops drawn together from all over the world has up to a point served to correct the one-sided disposition of power.

This brings us to a situation that has proved to be one of the major problems of the Council: the fact that on many subjects no free, preparatory theological discussion had taken place—not because the theologians had been gratuitously idle, but because they simply had not dared. After the encyclical *Humani generis* (1950), the give and take of theological argument on many important points of Christian doctrine and practice had come to a stop. Opposition to the Roman Curia, therefore—and to the Holy Office in particular—is not part of a campaign to drive the conservative elements out of the Church's administration; it is part of *a battle for freedom of speech,* for the possibility of an "open" conversation between progressives and conservatives. It witnesses to the conviction that, if the Church intends to be genuinely *catholic,* the elementary, free "civil rights" of her leading intellectuals must be secured.

An example: the sphere of morals

There are a number of highly placed conservatives in the ecclesiastical hierarchy who according to certain progressives and zealous reformists make a very poor showing indeed. From some of the accounts given one would gather that those who hold the highest offices and control the vital organs of government in the Church are a bevy of authoritarian, power-crazed megalomaniacs. Is that really so?

Cardinal Ottaviani has every appearance of being a charming and companionable man; and as for Fr Tromp—as anyone who has had contact with him knows—there is no getting away from the great earnestness with which this man envisages his task. One may, of course, be obliged to conclude that an individual here or there has acted in bad faith, or that one or other person displays the pathological symptoms of "authoritarian personality". But these are exceptions. Generally speaking, we have to do here with serious, hardworking people, fully conscious of their responsibilities. The trouble is that some of these leading figures are not aware of the great changes that have come about in the Church as a community, because they still base their outlook on an out-of-date conception of the Church and of the relationships and attitudes prevalent in it.

To illustrate this point, let us take a look at how the Church has understood herself in tackling the problem of Christian morals. The Church authorities saw it as their pastoral and parental task to mould the consciences of her children by giving the said children a detailed set of instructions and representing this as having the force of law. All this was based, of course, on the definite assumption that the Church was a community comprising a small group of experts wielding authority and a great mass of half-developed, immature Christian people. It is an ecclesial structure reproducing the features of medieval, feudal society.

Hence the hierarchical Church came to see herself as *Magistra ethicae*, the great instructress in Christian ethics. And she knew of no better way to discharge this function than by supplying an answer to every concrete moral problem, as and when it occurred. So the hierarchical Church thought that it could best inform the consciences of the faithful (that is, of the laity) by laying down detailed rules of moral conduct. Here we must point out that this attitude was shared and supported by the laity themselves. For it was not only the hierarchical Church that saw itself in this way. The faithful too found it quite natural that whether in or outside of the confessional they should be constantly putting before the clergy every possible kind of moral problem, in the most concrete and particular detail, and they believed that they had a *right* to clear pronouncements, answers and solutions.

But the centralized character of the Church was again a reason why the inferior clergy were not allowed to provide answers and solutions on their own responsibility. What answers and solutions they gave usually came not from themselves but from the moral theologians—and from the *auctores probati* at that! The moral theologians were in turn largely dependent on pronouncements made by higher ecclesiastical authority—if not, indeed, the highest of all: the pope himself. On ethical issues of major importance the pope's dicta were in fact the final word. Indeed, the charisma of infallibility, although officially restricted to *ex cathedra* declarations, was assumed to be operative in all other papal pronouncements, such as encyclicals, allocutions, briefs and *motu proprio* rescripts. Thus the Vatican I image of the Church, with its strong emphasis on infallibility and the central, unique authority of the pope, had its effect in the sphere of morals.

The important decisions which the pope took in this sphere were based on the counsel proffered by leading (Roman) moral theologians. These theologians did not let themselves be guided in their opinions by any consultation with laymen or by any attempt to examine the concrete social and human situation. But they arrived at their conclusions by deduction from "eternal verities and principles"; and in this they were much assisted by a particular notion of *natural law*. This natural law—often all too readily identified with divine law—was what gave rise to the existence of a sort of Christian "natural right". It was believed that "natural right" has a precisely definable content which is immutable and had to be formulated and endorsed by Church authority.

Once the pope had reached his decision or solution or

answer, then that started on its journey "downward". Moral theologians would try to refine further upon the papal formulas; and so there came into being those manuals of morality, voluminous yet for ever being revised and supplemented, dedicated to the strict letter of the law and heavy-laden with casuistry.

It was the job of the priest in the confessional to take the moral system arrived at in this way and apply it to actual "cases". "Apply" is hardly the word; for most cases were covered specifically by the casuistry supplied in the manual. All that the priests had to do was pass on the solution laid down or the answer prescribed. Apart from an enormous memory for detail, the business of the confessional really demanded relatively little of the priest in the way of independent thinking.

Here lies the nub of our problem today. The way in which the Church, in its guiding and governing rôle, saw to the moral nurture of the laity is now felt to have been overtaken by the new relationships prevailing within the Church as a community and by the whole development that has taken place in society itself. This is not to say that Christian morality has been left standing, so to speak—only the view of the Church which lay behind this particular pastoral technique or manner of putting the Church's pastoral concern into effect. It is chiefly those who have the "ordinary" cure of souls who are most painfully familiar with the problem and its ramifications; for it is they who are most immediately confronted with the concrete realities of the situation and know from intimate personal experience how untenable the traditional pastoral approach of the Church is in the sphere of morals. (We have particularly in mind here the moral issues associated with the sixth commandment and the whole question of marital ethics.) The bulk of the faithful no longer constitute an undifferentiated, semi-adult crowd of "common or garden believers". A lot of lay people are very much *au fait* with theological issues; and in the experience of many who are experts in one sphere or another the Church's way of approaching and dealing with these things is often in conflict with the confirmed results of pedagogic, psychological, sociological and demographic studies.

The hard core of the conflict lies in the fact that a certain sector of the Church—a sector wielding authority and power—still bases its outlook and behaviour on an outmoded picture of what the Church is like and understands herself to be—a picture that no longer tallies with the real state of affairs. Certainly it is still—as always—the job of the hierarchical Church to teach and preach in the Church with authority. But the question is how all this is to be envisaged within a Church community that in part at least has reached the age of discretion and responsibility. Perhaps we may put it like this: the hierarchical Church must now envisage her task of teaching and preaching as being to provide, in sustained dialogue with the faithful and with the whole existential world of reality as it is at present, guiding lines and principles with the aid of which we may all become mature believers, capable of making personal decisions of conscience in concrete situations and on the basis of our faith.

Catholicity inside the Church demands not only an open and healthy dialectic in the theological sector; perhaps even more important is the dialogue that should inform the relationship between hierarchy and layman. The layman hoped a great deal of the Council. But then we are confronted with the peculiar circumstance that a Council is chiefly an affair of the hierarchy. Is it—a Council—really an exhaustive representation of the whole Church? It is with this question in mind that we intend to concentrate in the second part of this chapter on the relation between office *(officium)* and charisma. This is a problem that touches home at many points on the plane of the hierarchy-layman relationship.

II. Office, Charisma and Layman in the Church

Every consideration of the nature of the Church or of particular aspects of the Church—such as catholicity—

brings to light truths often overlooked, which suddenly open up unforeseen perspectives. And so we would ask that some attention be given at this point to a theological discussion which started just prior to the first session of Vatican II. To be precise: it was the announcement that a Council was to be held that prompted various theologians to reflect upon the essential nature of an Ecumenical Council.

The legislation of the Code of Canon Law (can. 222–9) does not give a definition that might be treated in a dogmatic context; for the present legislation is not in line with the canonical structure of former councils. And so the question arises: what in fact *is* an Ecumenical Council?

The best known answer to this has been provided by the Tübingen theologian, Hans Küng, in his book *Structures of the Church.*[1] According to Küng, the Church is herself an Ecumenical Council, *called together by God*. This is deduced from the meaning of the New Testament terms for "Church" *(ecclesia)* and "calling" *(klesis)*. The *Ecclesia* is the assembly of *the called*, that is, of those called together by God—not just from Israel but from the whole of mankind. Ecumenical Councils, on the other hand, are called together *by men*. So then, the Council convened by men is a *representation* of the Council convened by God: the Church.[2]

General ecclesiastical Councils are thus *in essence* a "representation"—that is, "a reflection" and in some degree a "personification" of the Church, the Council called together by God (thus according to Küng "representation" here does not signify "substitution" or "deputizing", in the technical sense of "democratic representation").[3] Because the Council is a representation of the whole Church, Küng argues, it is not immediately self-evident that it is for bishops alone to participate in the Council. The absence of the laity must be seen as a particular historical development. Neither the synods of the early Church nor the Council of Nicaea nor again the reforming Councils of the Middle Ages were composed exclusively of bishops. Even the present canon law caters for the possibility of non-episcopal persons taking part in the Council (Abbots General and the Superiors General of Religious Orders). In Küng's view, then, it may be said that the bishops are eminently, but not exclusively, representative of the total Church.

This brings us to the question whether the layman should not have been present as a participant at this Council.

Finally, there remains the problem of the pope's position at a Council. Both in the Church and at a Council the special function of the Petrine office is to represent and guarantee the unity of the Church in the service of love and of the strengthening of faith. As we know from conciliar history—Küng says—very diverse forms of papal attendance can serve to fulfil this purpose; and one cannot say, *a priori*, that one of them is the ideal. We have to distinguish between a centre in the Church and papal centralism, between the need for a Petrine office and papalism.

The discussion widens

Küng's statement of his position brought a fairly speedy reaction from Professor Josef Ratzinger of Bonn University, who offered a number of critical comments on Küng's dogmatic analysis.[4] Ratzinger argued that a complete account of what a Council is is not to be had in terms of the "representation" idea. The essential structure of a Council cannot simply be inferred from the essential structure of the Church.

A Council represents the Church only under one particular aspect. The complete representation of the Church occurs *in the celebration of the Eucharist*, where people and pastors listen to the word of God and together consume the Bread of the Lord's Table. The Council, on the other hand, represents the Church principally with reference to the faith, in her function of proclaiming and maintaining the purity of the Gospel. We learn from Holy Scripture that Christ entrusted the preaching and due preservation of the Gospel message to the twelve apostles, whose successors are the members of the college of bishops. The Council is therefore not so much a representation-of-the-whole-Church (that being the Eucharist) as the practical implementation of the "collegiality" intrinsic to the essential character of the Church.

According to Ratzinger, therefore, the Council is no parliament and the bishops are not delegates. They represent in the first instance not the people but Christ, from whom they have received their mission and consecration. Thus they speak not on behalf of, or with the mandate of, the people, but of Christ. Ratzinger concedes that a theological justification has then still to be found for the participation of the non-episcopal members in the Council.

Although he does bring out some very important aspects, it must be said nonetheless that Ratzinger has not completely grasped what Küng means by "representation".

A valuable contribution from Karl Rahner

Professor Ratzinger's arguments brought the voice of a third party into the discussion: Karl Rahner. In an article entitled *Zur Theologie des Konzils*[5] Rahner likewise starts from the position that a Council is something other than a representation of the Church (on the one hand *more*, and on the other less). He goes on to develop some ideas which he had already put forward in a study of the collegial character of the episcopal office and its standing, structurally speaking, *vis-à-vis* the primacy.[6]

Mulling over the idea of "representation", he says: "The Church is structured and governed by the college of bishops with the pope as a 'personal apex'; but the essential nature of the Church is not exhaustively described in terms of this governing function with its institutional, hierarchical structure. To this essential character there belongs also the peculiarly *charismatic* element: that is, the gifts of the Spirit—intrinsic to the Church, certainly, but non-institutional—which are not just so much additional data to be regulated on a juridical basis" (p. 322).

What Rahner is trying to do here is to indicate the limited nature of a Council and to caution us against setting too much store by it. The total life of the Church does not consist, without remainder, in obediently acting upon and carrying out whatever the Church's "management" may decide. It is not because He sets to work in the highest governing circles of the Church that the Spirit of God is a'blowing. The Spirit bloweth where He listeth. So then, official authority in the Church may never claim sole possession of the Spirit. If that were the case, one would be bound, surely, to regard obedience to the ecclesiastical hierarchy as the supreme virtue.

Even if there were to have been lay people taking part in the Council, one would still—according to Rahner—not have a representation of the total nature of the Church; for the various charismata that pertain to her *Pleroma* (that is, to catholic fullness) cannot be adequately held within an institutional framework. And so it is actually impossible for the *whole* charismatic element in the Church to be represented at the Council. From this it follows that much of what is most vital in the Church by way of aspiration and desire (bearing, or seeming to bear, a charismatic stamp) was not ripe for the Council—at any rate, not yet. What the Council lacked of charisma it could not make up in decrees.

The charismatic element in the Church

In pointing with such emphasis to the fact that the charismatic element is part of the Church's essential character and that this could not be represented in all its fullness at the Council, Karl Rahner is indicating an important "forgotten truth". He preserves us from overestimating a Council on the assumption that the fullness of the Church is given expression in it; and he thereby saves us from possible later disappointment. But that is not all. Over and above that, he shows that a Council claiming for itself an absolute status, an unconditional authority of some kind, is not adequate to the challenge and demands of *catholicity*.

Rahner's highlighting of "the charismatic" acquires special significance in view of the current situation. There is a degree of opposition between the official and institutional aspect and the charismatic aspect in the Church. Of course, one must not exaggerate this contrast or make it absolute; for charisma is present in the Church's official governing authority—only not exclusively there. There is, however, one big—and very un-catholic—danger: that the official-institutional element may become so predominant in the Church that the charismata are hardly—or only with real difficulty— allowed their proper scope.

This happens whenever the official-cum-institutional element in the Church exhibits an inclination to regard itself as something absolute or lapses into being a "power machine", succumbs to a bureaucratic routine, comes to be an end in itself, begins to dominate instead of serving, dons a straitjacket of pure traditionalism and, in a mood of mingled anxiety and pride, insulates itself from new tasks and duties and from the exigencies of the time.[7] We do not say that things have gone as far as that; but what Pope Paul VI had to say about the Roman Curia did suggest that the danger was not an imaginary one and that, as things had developed, there was a tendency for the official, institutional element to set too much store by itself.

The power to command in the Church must not be taken to mean that, as in a totalitarian system, the ecclesiastical authority can and should plan every undertaking and activity there on an autocratic basis. God sometimes desiderates and demands certain activities and movements even *before* ecclesiastical officialdom has given the starting-signal.[8] Ecclesiastical authority must not aspire, therefore, to keep every charismatic or prophetic movement in leading-strings all the time; but it must acknowledge all charismatically inspired wisdom coming "from below" and must be open to its influence.

We have the impression that in the past the charismatic element in the Church has not always been able to find its rightful place, that it has often had to go "underground" or has even been "quenched". We use this last expression advisedly; for was it not St Paul himself who pointed to the danger of "quenching" the Spirit? It is a matter of the greatest concern that the charismata, the special gifts of the Spirit, should get a proper chance to be recognized and should not be suffocated through a lack of comprehension or by mental sloth, clerical *amour propre* or a surrounding atmosphere of sheer hostility, even in the Church itself.[9]

If we cease to be open to the charismatic and take our stand in the Church on the official and institutional side alone, then faith is in danger of being dried up and withered. Nothing is more inimical to a living faith than the consciousness that everything is already "wrapped up" in dogmatic formulas and legal prescripts and the knowledge that, if there is anything not yet wrapped up in this way, it will be settled for us along the customary institutional lines. We must all recover a sense of the inexhaustible mystery of God's word and the mysterious operation of his Spirit. If we do not, we shall land ourselves—as in the time of Samuel—in a period of spiritual dearth: "and the word of the Lord was precious in those days, and there was no open vision".[10]

We have tried to point to some of the dangers that currently threaten catholicity within the Church: a certain exclusivist theology, which cannot tolerate healthy theological controversy and the free expression of opinion; attempts to apply ecclesiastical censorship in order to impose a uniform style of thinking and of formulating doctrine in the Church; a clinging to an outmoded image of the Church; a fondness for insisting that decision-making be centralized and all decisions taken "at the top"; a disregard for the charismatic element in the Church; and, finally, a temptation to see a Council as an exhaustive representation of the whole Church.

How would the Church look if these limitations on her internal catholicity were not there? We do not know. It is for us to continue, in an attitude of faith, to be receptive and ready for what is to come. Our enduring task is to be "catholic" and to make the Church eventualize.

V

Catholicity and Morals

That these two words should be coupled together may at first sight strike one as being rather strange. We are concerned with discovering what the implications of catholicity are inside the Church; and in the previous chapter a number of observations have been made already on the way that an un-Catholic mentality can impede the proper business of theologizing. It is of the greatest interest here to investigate theology, so far as its content and purpose are concerned, taking the principle of catholicity as one's starting-point. In this chapter we want to do this, but confining our attention to an aspect presented by the field of *morals*. And this will not involve our examining what the official moral theology of the Church teaches. Our job will be to stick to the hard facts and to concern ourselves with life as it really is.

A "catholic" morality really must relate to the whole life of the Christian. That much is a *sine qua non* for any morality that claims to be universal, all-embracing—in a word, "catholic".

For a start, let us hear what the German novelist and polemical writer, Heinrich Böll, has to say. In his "Letter to a young Catholic" he addresses himself to a youthful recruit just back from a retreat: "They will have warned you there about the moral pitfalls of a soldier's life, and—as is usual with this sort of admonition—identified morality, as always, with sexual morality. I will not weary myself by expatiating for your benefit on the enormous theological error inherent in such an identification. The whole of European Catholicism has been labouring under this one-sided interpretation of morality for the best part of a century."[1]

That is a pretty stiff accusation: that morality in a

Catholic context is identified with sexual morality. Even the compilers of the most traditional textbooks on the subject could point out that this is not true. But Heinrich Böll is talking here not about the textbooks but about actual experience, pastoral practice and the moral consciousness of the average Catholic. We may feel entitled to put the question again, however: is this true? Some people are inclined to say that it was perhaps true not so very long ago, but that to put it that way nowadays would be going too far.

I. The Current "Embarras de Conscience"

It is not at all easy, of course, to get an overall view of pastoral practice and of the moral consciousness of the average Catholic. At this point I can only rely, therefore, on my own practice as a confessor, checking it against my conversations with other priests who regularly hear a great number of confessions.

For the average confessor the periods round about Easter and Christmas, when the hearing of confessions is on a large scale, are especially instructive on this score. From the chaotic picture presented by such a variety of confessions there does gradually emerge a vast pattern of sins, inner conflicts, misgivings and scruples and a certain sense of guilt. And from all this it would appear that for far and away the greater number of the faithful, Christian morality does boil down to the morality of sexual conduct. The pattern of sins relates mainly to the following: masturbation, casual promiscuity, "taking liberties" and sexual intercourse during courtship and betrothal, abnormal marital relations in connection with birth-control, marital infidelity occasioned by an unsatisfactory relationship between man and wife. Not only has the moral consciousness been narrowed down to this sort of thing, but one is bound to say that the feeling of guilt about such matters assumes abnormal proportions, while at the same time neurotic or semi-neurotic anxieties are manifested.

All this helps to undermine the value of confession as a sacrament. The confessional could well be described, perhaps, as an encounter within the fellowship of the Church with the forgiving Christ, or as an effectuation through Church and sacrament of God's mercy and lovingkindness. Instead of this, however, the confessor has forced upon him in the confessional the rôle of therapeutist and dispenser of mental hygiene—a function for which he is by no means always well suited. Particularly at "religious peak periods" such as Easter and Christmas the priest in the confessional is confronted with a great mass of Catholics who fancy themselves on the periphery of normal Catholic church life. They are conscious that for the most part they are unable to live up to the standards of Catholic morality (for which read: sexual morality). Some are still hopeful; others have, practically speaking, given up. They carry on in a more or less vague state of "bad conscience", the awareness of which is now to the forefront and now very much at the back of their minds. They know that they are living in mortal sin and so are excluded from the Eucharistic sacrament and presumably from eternal salvation.

They pin their hopes on the last sacraments: that is, they hope that in mortal extremity they will still be able to make their confession in time and so, albeit by the skin of their teeth, reach eternity in a state of absolution. These are the folk—and there are many of them—who want to spend Easter and Christmas relieved, temporarily at any rate, of the pangs of a troubled conscience, or who go to confession prior to a lengthy trip abroad by car or to a journey by air.

One can see here an evident devaluation not only of the sacrament of confession but of the Eucharist as well. The fact is that according to this way of looking at things taking one's part in the Eucharist is interpreted simply and solely as a token that one has been a good, church-fearing Christian, and as a kind of reward for complying with the norms of Catholic morality.

Confession is reduced to the level of an institution designed for the (temporary) relief of troubled consciences and oppressive guilt-feelings. Just one more start with the slate clean—this people must have, even when they know that it cannot possibly stay clean for long. This often proves to be the beginning of the road to a "churchless" kind of living: people feel or come to realize that confession when treated like this makes no sense. They already feel themselves excluded from the Eucharist, anyway. When the confessional too ceases to offer an anchorage or any lasting comfort, this sacrament loses all real value. And so the whole pursuit of life within the membership of the Church is thrown over—either suddenly or in gradual stages—as being pointless and as offering no solid prospect.

This is not an unfair or pessimistic picture of the way things are. It is based to begin with on my personal experiences as a pastor; and my many conversations with both priests and lay people have served to verify the rest.

The official moral code and the real situation

Now I come to what I really wish to propose. I am not concerned here with what constitutes the Catholic code of morals, but with the actual, existential state of affairs: the way in which morals are lived out *in fact*.

Well now, if Catholic morality is in fact and for very much the greater part restricted to sexual morality and dominated by abnormal feelings of anxiety and guilt, *then what we have to deal with is in point of fact an unauthentic, false, infantile, even un-Christian moral system*. We must at once add: a morality that conflicts with the principle of catholicity. It is an aspect of the depth-dimension of catholicity that is in question here: a Catholic morality, in actual fact and not just in theory, must address *the whole man* and not simply one particular facet of his existence.

From these assertions some painful conclusions must be drawn: that there is an alarming deficiency in our preaching of Christian morality and an equally alarming vacuum in our pastoral practice, which has not succeeded in breaking through the narrow limits of moral consciousness and in alleviating the distress of conscience which generally prevails.

Then one wonders how such a development—or stagnation, rather—could possibly have come about. Has the sometimes diffuse anxiety of the celibate about sexual matters led to a narrowing of the pastoral counsellor's own mental outlook? Has the elaborate casuistry of the textbooks had the effect of paralysing all initiative and independent thinking on how to tackle moral problems? Has a juridical and legalistic approach so permeated our morality as to obscure our view of the ethics of the Gospel? There are a lot of questions here. It will not do to put the blame on hard-pressed spiritual advisers. We are probably *all* the victims of a tendency, a frame of mind and outlook, an upbringing within the climate of Catholic life, that has impaired and weakened our sensitivity to the real moral demands and challenges of the Gospel.

It is pointless, however, to affirm all these things, unless we go on to ask ourselves: what should we be doing about it?

I would want to define our task in these terms: *to seek for a morality that will be truly catholic and genuinely based on the Gospel*—a morality that at the same time will speak to the condition of modern man and the world of his experience; a morality enunciated in a way that he can understand and that is going to command his attention.

In the next section we shall first consider what must be done prior to any renewal of Christian morality, what risk must be undertaken, so that we can then indicate in what perspective we may have to conduct our search for the authentically "catholic" morality of the Gospel.

II. Attempts to Alleviate the Acute Perplexity of Conscience

There has been no shortage of effort on the part of moral theologians at a high academic level to look for solutions to the moral problems that we have just been particularizing.

But these moral theologians have often been hamstrung by the lack of freedom which until recently prevailed in the sphere of Catholic theological thinking. Any lines in moral theology that were unduly novel could not be pursued without exposing oneself to official—or officious—accusations of heresy.

Consequently, the first remedies have been sought out and applied by those who are themselves involved in a pastoral ministry and have had the most direct experience of the perplexity felt by many Catholics.

The "easy" way out

There are spiritual advisers, moved by sympathy and an honest-to-goodness concern at the distress and anxiety of mind and conscience felt by so many people, who have supposed that the answer lies with an attitude of thoroughgoing permissiveness. This has meant that instead of insisting on the rigorous application of moral principles as currently received, they have swung to the other extreme. They have tried to cure the morbid "guilt complex" by making light of certain acts or by arguing the guilt and sinfulness attaching to them out of existence. Thus it was said of masturbation that this was a normal sexual reaction which ought not to be suppressed and that therefore masturbation could not be any sort of reason for disquiet. Some even contended that this did not need to be confessed, since it had nothing to do with a person's relation to God. Lovers or engaged couples who had sexual intercourse were advised at any rate to do it "for love". Married people whom circumstances had prompted to adopt certain contraceptive practices were told that, placed as they were, this was all right for them and morally quite acceptable.

This kind of solution did generally afford some temporary relief, of course; but for many penitents it turned out in the longer term to be unsatisfying. The confessors who—with the best of intentions, be it said—adopted this extreme, minimalizing approach to the consciousness of sin failed to reckon with something that human beings generally find to be part of their experience. What we have in mind here is this: every person is more or less aware of what he ought, *qua* human being, to be, and at the same time he knows experientially that he is always falling short of that quality of being. *Mutatis mutandis*, this holds good for the Christian individual with respect to the moral demands made on him as a Christian. Now it is this experience of continually falling short of what is required, ethically speaking, which gives rise to the further experience of *being guilty*, of being a sinner. Confession is designed to meet this authentically human condition and experience. It invites the individual to acknowledge his guilt and to pray for forgiveness. The Church, represented by the priest, pronounces absolution in the name of Christ and at his behest. She can do this because Christ is the Lamb of God who has taken upon him the sins of the world. Each confession is thus a proleptic appropriation of that final deliverance which the end of the Age will bring, when man is not only set free from his sins but is also delivered from his condition of being a sinner.

It is an illusion, however, to imagine that man can be totally and finally delivered from his "being in guiltiness" during this life. That definitive and total deliverance is granted us only in the Age-to-come. To be in guilt—or, if you will, to be in sin—is part and parcel of man's existence here and now. If never to dirty our hands is what we want, we shall have to stop being humans.

To return to our problem: we have to say that the clergy of whom we have been speaking made the mistake of thinking that in order to cure people of a one-sided, morbid and neurotic guilt-complex one could dispense with a sense of guilt altogether. But this leaves the human person who feels or knows that he is in fact guilty a prey to conflict and confusion; and he feels too that somehow he is not being taken quite seriously. However well intentioned, therefore, this method of dealing with the problems specified seems to me to be wrong.

A more responsible way of dealing with concrete difficulties

On what lines, then, is a proper and satisfying solution to be sought? It has long been an accepted principle in morals that the circumstances, the situation within which a sin is committed, can alter the character of the sin and extenuate the guilt. Maybe we would reach a better solution of the problems under consideration if we understood better the situation in which the man of today finds himself and if we knew more about the real nature of these sexual problems. That on the one hand. On the other, we must learn to appreciate the fact that a man needs time if he is to attain a certain ethical standard. The truth is that in the ethical sphere—*especially* there—there must be scope for development.

This approach would seem to offer a more acceptable solution in the situation that we have been describing. At all events, it enables one to take a charitable view, without having to rationalize out of existence the consciousness of guilt which people have.

We will now take a number of concrete difficulties and show what the practical solutions are that are being offered.

1. *Masturbation*. Pastors and spiritual advisers do not need to have read the *Kinsey Report* to know that masturbation is common not only among young people but with a lot of adults as well. We have only now got hold of the idea that masturbation is partly the consequence of an excessive preoccupation of society with sex. If the puritanism of earlier generations tended to hush up the fact of sexuality and, so to speak, sweep it under the carpet, in our time this has given way—owing perhaps to a measure of reaction—to an often unwholesome exhibitionism. Then again, commercial advertising has been only too glad to exploit sex as a means of catching and holding attention. The younger generation especially are thus subjected during the years of puberty to powerful and multifarious sexual stimuli. Instead of there being a gradual development, sexual maturity is coming about sometimes with great speed and with startling

suddenness. But, aside from these social causes of masturbation, we now have more of an idea of what the thing is in itself.

In the first place, one has to distinguish between onanism during puberty and onanism in later life. In puberty it is often bound up with the discovery of one's own physical nature, which is experienced during this stage of life in a new way. Sexuality makes its presence felt; but it is felt as a mysterious something-or-other secluded within one's own body. Onanism in puberty, therefore, will often be a way of trying to discover the secret of one's own sexuality. By the time it is getting to be something of a habit, the onanist has a vague suspicion that he is not exercising his sexuality in accordance with its proper meaning. He is using his sexual function in order to love *himself*, as it were; and to that extent onanism is a sign of infantilism and egocentrism. Often there is a fixation on the new "discovery", which results in the young person's losing all interest in other matters. He shuts himself off from his parents and becomes something of an introvert.

The spiritual counsellor will have to show a great deal of understanding here and try to free the youngster from his self-enclosure and isolation. The immensely exciting and captivating experience of masturbation and the sense of frustration which ensues directly after the act sometimes arouse severe guilt-feelings. The confessor will not try to explain these away, but will make an attempt to lead the young person concerned to understand the true significance of his "discovery". The term "mortal sin" will no longer come into it; but the point will be made that what he—or she—is doing is not right and that what God desires is that he or she will learn to put these new powers to the use which he has ordained for them. The youngster will be counselled not to confess masturbation with undue frequency and will often be permitted to receive Holy Communion even without raising the issue in the confessional. In that case, of course, they are to make, *prior* to communion, a heartfelt, personal act of repentance. The vital point here is that there should be a pastoral method and approach aimed at really helping young persons and bringing them on, thereby ensuring that the sense of guilt does not get out of proportion and that it does not remain fixated on this one thing.

Masturbation at a later period, it would appear, is seldom the outcome of sheer perversity—of the urge to obtain merely sensual pleasure or gratification. It is generally to be met with among people trying to compensate in some way: those unable to satisfy their natural affectivity, those who are subject to contactual disturbances and are incapable of breaking out of their isolation. Here again there is a better understanding on the counsellor's part of what he is about. The right approach to this, from a pastoral standpoint, requires us to take a generous and charitable view and to seek to track down the real sources of the trouble.

2. *Free behaviour or sexual intercourse during courtship* ought likewise to be set in a proper light—that is, in the light of the situation. I certainly get the impression that young people are more keen on the affective contact which happens during a protracted courtship than on getting married. There is an ever widening gap between the attainment of sexual maturity and the possibility of marriage; and this is why courtship tends to be of increasing importance and to last longer. It is becoming a period in which the element of preparation for marriage is played down in favour of the pursuit of sexual experiences, secondary or primary. It is in any case not surprising that during such a long period of courtship things do not always stop at "a kiss and a cuddle", as the saying goes. The confessor is not going to approve sexual intercourse in these circumstances; but he will show very much more understanding of the difficulties encountered by these young people.

In the first place, the whole social and economic set-up does make an early marriage extremely difficult. The demands made on a young man *before* he can establish himself in society with any degree of independence are often very high; and it takes much longer than it used to do for him to complete his studies or apprenticeship, or get his diploma or degree. Furthermore, there is a major handicap in the critical *housing shortage,* which means that it is no longer rare for the engagement period to extend over anything up to seven or eight years. It is possible that what needs to be exposed here is a sinful structure in our society. Has our government not opted, after all, for the housing shortage, at the expense of the wellbeing of many young people?

The confessor is not likely to have any cut-and-dried answers up his sleeve to the problems created by lengthy courtships. Yet he must guard against any tendency to wink at such conduct or even to condone it. He will be bound to point out that, where intercourse is concerned, marriage itself demands certain sacrifices. Having to wait a long time before the marriage is not in itself a calamity; an unhappy or broken marriage is. Demanding an absolute right to sexual intercourse before the knot has been finally tied (for the most part, a typically male attitude) already suggests that true love has fallen somewhere by the wayside. "Education for loving", therefore, is very important; but that is quite a different thing, of course, from palming off a frustrated couple, eager for marriage, with the pastoral "stone-waller": "try and think of it as a modest sacrifice on your part."

3. Lastly, we shall take a brief look at the question of *birth-control* (in an excursus at the end of the chapter we shall come back to this subject in more detail).

Those engaged in the pastoral ministry are of course especially grateful for the comforting words uttered by Bishop Bekkers in his televised address of 21 March 1963. This episcopal pronouncement has been variously judged; but at least it has been clear to us that if the bishop was outspoken it was through a genuine pastoral concern, and that he courageously gave expression to what many directly engaged in a pastoral ministry were already putting into practice. There are a lot of reasons why the prospect of increasing one's family can become quite a problem for married people nowadays. There is, for example, the medical issue: the doctor says that there ought to be no more children. Or again, there are considerations of a psychic character: tremendous fear of a further pregnancy, abnormal nervous tension or inability on the woman's part to cope with a horde of small children. There is the financial factor too: another child would put an unjustifiable strain on the family's financial resources. There are many other reasons as well, such as having to live in a tiny flat: there is literally no room for another child.

Situations like these constrain married couples to use birth-control. In the traditional moral teaching the physical cohabitation of man and wife comes to be viewed far too much in isolation from the aspect of love in marriage. It was maintained that if no more children could be permitted to come, sexual intercourse must simply stop. The love between the couple would then become something more spiritual and so would actually be improved. People who could not abstain from sexual intercourse were instructed to carry on as usual, in that case, and to trust to divine Providence—a celebrated pastoral stopgap!

Confessors have again come to understand better the implications of the fact that the physical side of marriage is inextricably bound up with marital affection and indeed supports and stimulates it; and they have realized that one cannot call a halt to sexual intercourse without doing damage to the totality of the marriage. What are the couples to do for whom birth-control has become an imperative need? Periodic abstention can be a way out; but there are a lot of difficulties attaching to it, and many people find that for practical and technical or psychological reasons they cannot pursue this form of continence. For the way towards a solution we may cite Bishop Bekkers: "We realize that there are situations in which it is impossible to take account of all Christian and human values at one and the same time. The Church knows that well-intentioned concern for their family and for each other leads married people to follow courses which the Church may not acknowledge to be right. But then the Church also knows that she must allow room for a gradual, and indeed at times tardy and imperfect, growth, such as exists also in other areas of the moral life: love of one's neighbour, candour, honesty and so forth".[2]

In practical terms, what does the pastor do now? He will point out, perhaps, that the decision regarding birth-control in a marriage may be arrived at on real, and not fictitious or pretended, grounds. So far as various methods of preventing conception are concerned, he will say that these are not proper, but that in *this* marriage, under *these* particular circumstances, what is normally required of a marriage in its moral aspect is not feasible. He will explain that in this situation one is not to think in terms of a mortal sin; for if in spite of this enforced lack of completeness in their married life the couple nevertheless try in everything to be honest Christians, there is no question of their being bereft of God's friendship. For this reason he permits them to receive Holy Communion without having to go to confession every time.

We have outlined in some detail what is being done at the moment here and there in the pastoral sphere with the aim of easing, in a measure, the conscience of many a sorely troubled Catholic. Doubtless there is still a great deal to be done and a great deal that still needs to be thought over carefully. The first thing is to get rid of abnormal guilt-feelings and neurotic pangs of conscience; but still more important is to overcome the fixation, in the moral sphere, on matters of sex. *This has to be done first,* if the way is to be clear to forming conscience so that it will now cover *the whole field* of Christian moral conduct in its existential setting of reality. Only then can we properly speak of a "catholic" moral system—one, that is to say, which is authentically Christian.

III. Perspectives of an Authentic Christian Morality

The catholicity of Christian morality will always be constricted and impoverished under the influence of legalism or of a legalistic moral system, so-called. The struggle with the notion of morality as a code of law is nothing new; and in our own time it is being waged with both integrity and enthusiasm. But even if the most conspicuous excrescences and outcrops of legalism in the moral sphere have been pruned away, it is always there in the undercurrent of thinking about morals and in actual experience. And this is what we must take up now.

The victory over legalism

By legalism or a legalistic moral system we mean the idea that morality is a mere matter of conformity to externally imposed rules.[3] Whether a given activity or mode of behaviour is good or bad simply depends on whether it does or does not accord with the rule. The inner disposition of the agent is either a secondary matter or is considered in isolation and as having little to do with the case. The motive for keeping to the rule is fear of the sanctions which operate if the rule is not followed. We are in the realm of the purely juridical here; and that means that every human action is rendered *measurable*, so to speak. The action is "measured" against the rule; and then all is clear—the thing is good or bad.

What we find, then, in Christian morality is a recrudescence of pharisaism which is quite happy with a punctilious, purely outward observance of the law; and pharisaism or legalism is at all times a danger and a threat to Christian morality. In our own day the systematized and casuistical method of the textbooks on morals has generated a kind of neo-pharisaism. It is certainly true that the manuals were not intended originally as expositions of Christian morality, but as practical guides for the confessor. In fact, these books of instruction have gradually come to be revered as *the*

Christian moral code; and so they have become the source of a new kind of legalism that via the confessional and the pulpit has more and more permeated the moral consciousness of the ordinary Catholic.

Not only is the morality of a person's conduct measured by the rule—as the legalistic notion requires—but moral judgment becomes a matter of measurement too—notably in the way the categories of mortal and venial sin are so expertly manipulated. By employing these categories it is possible to ascertain who is eternally lost and who is not. One outcome—among others—of this is that remarkable figure of the man who makes a regular thing of confessing mortal sins and is therefore at one moment a lost soul and at the next numbered among the elect.

In what, then, does the great error of legalism consist? In this: that the ethical norms, in so far as they are formulated, acquire an existence of their own, in detachment from the human person as subject. These norms turn into, as it were, an "eternal" order of things inscribed upon the very firmament of heaven and constraining man to obedience. If it be asked whence comes this unconditional demand, the only possible reply is one or other variation on the theme of "orders is orders". Thus legalism is blind to the fact that man is *himself a light*—a *lumen naturale*—that shines in this world and attains to self-comprehension in the process. In that light, which in some way or other he himself is, man learns to understand himself as a "subject" that must realize itself through its operating in and upon this world and still more through the encounter with others. This light-which-is-man has not contrived to cast a swift and clear illumination over every single norm. It has been a long, evolutive process. Only step by step has man come to see in the course of his dialectical contact with the world and with his fellows the ethical norms assigned to his existence *qua* human being. Thus in this process he has learned that he is not free to annihilate with impunity his fellow man, to destroy his life and personality; and this is expressed in the formula: "Thou shalt not kill." At a later stage of ethical consciousness man came to see that to "be human" means "having to be for others", means "having others as one's true end and destiny".[4] And then it is but one step to saying: we must love and cherish our fellow men. But man has never got very far with this last ethical demand—with seeing and understanding it in all its universality—apart from some disclosure that comes to him with the authority of God.

The moral implications of the Gospel

This critique of legalism, both manifest and concealed, was necessary, if only to bring us to the question of the morality intrinsic to the Gospel; and to that question we now turn.

When God enters history in the person of Jesus Christ, morality has ceased, for the Jewish people, to be anything more than a kind of legalism. The course of Jesus' life is very largely ordered by the battle which he wages against this legalism in its pharisaic form; and Paul is to carry on this struggle in his letters, using Jewish theology itself for that purpose.

The moral implications of the Gospel must be understood in their context, which is the annunciation of the Kingdom of God. That Kingdom is the inauguration of his dominion in this world. His loving, gracious and saving dominion, however, is not one that imposes itself by *force majeure* and overwhelms us because it is irresistible; but it is a dominion, a kingdom, into which we are *invited* and into which we can enter in freedom.

What then must people do to belong to this Kingdom? They must *believe*. For believing is the basic Christian stance —a basically theo–logical one—which arises from our being addressed by the Word of God and stirred up by God's Spirit, and comes about through our response: a turning and a surrender of the whole man to the person of Jesus Christ, his saving activity and his Good News. This reality is described by Mark as follows: "Now after John was arrested, Jesus came into Galilee, preaching the Gospel of God, and saying, 'The time is fulfilled, and the Kingdom of God is at hand; repent, and believe in the Gospel' " (Mark 1. 14–15).

What is being spoken of here is actually something new in the ethical realm: belief requires a *metanoia*, a conversion. The word "conversion" is not an adequate rendering of the Greek *metanoia*, which signifies a radical change of heart, with a positive stress on the inward disposition: a radical alteration or transformation of one's state of mind and outlook. We are too much inclined to conceive of "belief" and *metanoia* as momentary, once-for-all occurrences; but in fact there are many stages of both—and one may say that the moral life of the Christian is bound to be a continuous *metanoia* and a process of growth in believing.

The Sermon on the Mount and the new commandment

Is Jesus a revolutionary, that is, one who would put something new in place of all that has gone before, throwing the past overboard and proclaiming a totally new ethical attitude to life? No. Jesus is not a revolutionary, but a radical renovator, a "renewer": that is, he wants to renew everything from its *radix*, its root. That root is the Jewish Law, which Christ has no intention, he says, of abrogating. Nevertheless, the Jewish Law is evidently imperfect—not to say defective; and our Lord shows clearly what that imperfection is in the Sermon on the Mount, a disclosure that might well be described as the moral programme of Christ.

Now the great weakness of the Jewish Law is that it can be taken all too easily in a legalistic sense. And so at the beginning of the Sermon on the Mount Christ says: Unless your righteousness is something better than the legalistic attitude which passes for righteousness with the Pharisees, the Kingdom is not for you. After this passage there follows a remarkable series of sayings, all beginning with the words: "You have heard that it was said . . ."; and then comes a quotation from the Jewish Law, followed by an exclamatory

"But *I* say unto you . . .". In the final part of the sentence the commandment, whatever it may be, is re-expressed in a form intensified to an unlimited degree. One example must suffice: "You have heard that it was said to the men of old, 'You shall not kill; and whoever kills shall be liable to judgment'. But I say to you that every one who is angry with his brother shall be liable to judgment" (Matt. 5. 21, 22).

In saying this kind of thing Christ means to make it clear to us that our Christianity will be barren, if we set about it in a legalistic and minimalizing spirit. Our ethical attitude must be: always be ready to aim for the highest and the best. This insistence on the *maximal* must not put us off or cripple our determination; but it will of course put paid to moral complacency of any sort.[5]

It has been necessary to take a fresh look at the Christian ethic—as unfolded in the Sermon on the Mount—in order to arrive at the crucial issue: the proclamation of the culminating point of Christian morality, which is the command to love, to love one's neighbour. Now the proclamation of the commandment to love as being the first and great commandment is something with which we are not unfamiliar. Indeed, it is a commonplace of our religion. It has become almost a pastoral platitude.

We consider that love for the neighbour needs to be presented afresh today as the centre and culmination of a catholic morality; because an insidious legalism, abnormal feelings of anxiety and guilt and a fixation on sexual matters have obscured, if they have not rendered entirely opaque, the true significance of this commandment. It may be that we no longer even know what it means in the practical sphere of Christian living to say that love is the first and great commandment.

Misunderstanding of the command to love

How has the meaning of the first commandment become clouded like this? The best way of answering that question is, I think, to give a few examples.

1. The command to love one's neighbour runs as follows: "You are to love your neighbour as yourself." Now these last words, "as yourself", are taken to be the standard, the *measure*, of neighbourly love. See, for instance, a modern moral theologian like Bernhard Häring *(The Law of Christ*, vol. II, 1962, p. 377). C. A. Damen in his *Theologia moralis* (Rome 1950, I, no. 350) does even worse. This writer says emphatically that love for one's neighbour is limited—and rightly so—by consideration for oneself. I must not cherish my neighbour if, in consequence, I am going to compromise my own perfection.

The love displayed by Christ on the cross radically contradicts this view; but this type of moralist sees the love of one's neighbour as, in the last analysis, a means of adding to one's own virtue, or in other words as ultimately doing one's own "I" a good turn. In this way, framed within a more or less legalistic turn of mind, love of the neighbour gets hedged round once more—and in fact we actually hear talk of the "measure" of neighbourly love, and so forth. Here we would object that the words "as yourself" do not refer to any measure of the love in question, or to the degree of its intensity, or to the manner of it. Love of one's neighbour has to do with an existential, and not a predicamental, relationship: a turning in love towards the other, a commitment without bounds or conditions. The meaning, therefore, of the commandment can be expressed in these terms (after a striking interpretation offered by Martin Buber): in your being good, relate yourself to the other as though he were you.

2. We are to love our neighbour *because he is our neighbour*. But it is often said that we must love our neighbour "for God's sake"; and this is explained or justified more or less as follows: cherishing one's neighbour is a means to loving God. The assumption is that God must be the direct object of our love and the neighbour a means to this love of God—which is as much as to say: ultimately an aid to our own sanctity. As I see it, this is not really loving one's neigh-

bour at all; for in all Christian love of the neighbour he is *himself*, as a person, the object of such love, and not a corridor to God. God has shown us in Christ what love is; and through his word and his Spirit we are enabled to make that love visible again on earth. Consequently, to love in this sense means: to enter into God's saving activity, seeing that love is always redemptive.

3. Love for one's neighbour applies not merely to relationships between persons, but must also interpenetrate the social, political and economic structures of our society and of the world in which we live together. In so far as a society remains structured by the heritage of a liberal capitalism, it is structured on unchristian, love-less principles of profit and competition.

Moreover, we live in a world where seventeen per cent of the population own or control eighty per cent of the wealth. That portion of the world in which this wealth is concentrated is in fact very largely inhabited by Christians. Would this not suggest, then, that the Christians with their ethic of love are not present in this world to very much effect?[6]

Grossouw has pointed out already that Christ detected a tremendous moral danger not in things sexual but in the monetary realm[7]—not because wealth is in itself a bad thing but because it so easily causes a man to shut his heart against his fellows and becomes an idol that excludes the service of the true God. An ethics of love confronts us with world-encompassing (catholic) demands, the implications of which were obscured by the traditional morality. Now, however, we are just about beginning once more to have an inkling as to what they are.

Towards a new morality

It is not our task here to propound a new ethics, based on the command to love. Our business in this chapter is simply to point to the defective, and thus disquieting, way in which morality is actually understood and practised. At the same time we want to open up a prospect of renewal for Christian morality. I am firmly convinced that this prospect is to be sought in a radical reform of our moral ideas and behaviour, on the basis of the first commandment.

In order to call attention effectively to this we may even have to trail our coat and assert that in the Christian ethic one thing and one thing only is prescribed—namely, love—and that the only intrinsic evil is a lack of love.[8] Not that this is so very new, however; for it was Augustine who said: "*Dilige et quod vis fac*"—love, and do what you will. It may look as though a morality deriving from this simple principle gives *carte blanche* to (moral) libertinism. The fact is that a morality motivated by love makes far higher demands than the traditional morality which is steeped in legalism.

To the young man who contemplates having certain sexual relations with his girl friend and asks himself "Why not?", it is easy enough to say: it is wrong, it is sin. But it is much harder to come up with an answer to the question: Do you really love her . . . or do you covet rather than love her? To covet, to desire, is an affective urge centred on the "ego"; but to love is to "give" yourself to the other without hidden motives of any kind. If the young man is then in all honesty compelled to recognize that he covets his girl friend rather than loves her, he will have to admit that in terms of a morality based on love his action is an immoral one. If he really loves the girl, he will respect her too much to "make use" of her or permit himself to take liberties with her.[9]

"Give yourself in love" is a simple-seeming recommendation which in fact conceals just how difficult Christian love of one's neighbour is. Freud may well have been right when he said that evil consists entirely in the fact that we are afraid really to give ourselves to the other and that this fear wears the mask of morality.

The moral precepts of Jesus in the Sermon on the Mount are therefore not to be taken in a spirit of legalism. They are not a piece of legislation setting out plainly what love requires of you on each and every occasion. No; the Sermon merely shows us, by way of illustration, what love *could* demand, now or at any time, of any and every individual. In that sense one can say that love is the only real commandment that Christ has given us. But it is never susceptible of being pinned down in a system of casuistry or in a more detailed set of instructions. Every situation in life, therefore, requires the Christian, starting from the commandment to love, to *create* his moral stance and the course of action that he is going to pursue. Thus existence for the Christian is no "prescribed" existence. The Christian must always be "projecting" his existence, with love as his point of departure.

Just one more thought to end with: love of one's neighbour is not the same as a humanistic love of mankind in general. To the question as to who is my neighbour, Christ has replied with inimitable simplicity in the parable of the Good Samaritan. There it is clearly this or that particular person, my fellow man *in concreto*, whom I encounter in a concrete situation. Potentially, all men are my neighbours. Because of the means of communication that we have today, the encounter between a man and his fellows is far more differentiated than in earlier times. An encounter is no longer necessarily a matter of physical proximity; and we must bear in mind too that socio-economic structures are structures of encounter.

It is evident, therefore, that, as in other respects, "catholicity" in the sphere of Christian morals implies that an exacting task is laid upon us—one which so far is being fulfilled in only a very limited sense. A genuine "catholic" morality proceeds from love of our fellow man, whoever he may be; and the love here—the love intended by Christ—is universal, all-embracing, that is to say *catholic*. Potentially, no one is to be excluded from this love. Consequently, it is positively immoral to treat persons or groups of persons as demonic—which is just what we do when we refer, for instance, to the communists or their leaders as "the devil" or as "antichrist". Would not the world assume a very different look if Christians were to take seriously the universality of love?

The perspective needed for this is fundamentally incomplete; the new morality still has to be written up. But life is always ahead of our formulated reflections. That is why I hope that many people, inspired by their religion and the consciousness of what it implies, are already *living out* what I have so laboriously been trying to articulate.

IV. An Excursus on the Question of Birth-Control

We shall end this chapter by taking a look at the problem of birth-control. It may at first sight seem strange that within the framework we have proposed a relatively detailed problem of marital ethics should have a section all to itself. But then we have to remember that every problem in morals, however detailed—if one wants to handle it at a fundamental level—presupposes and invokes the whole scheme of morality. For this reason it seemed useful, against the background of the ideas and perspectives unfolded in this chapter, to examine a contemporary problem and attempt to elucidate it. Among other things, we shall see to what extent the question of birth-control raises issues directly connected with what we have been saying about the central place of love in Christian morality.

Over-estimating sexuality

The whole nexus of problems relating to birth-control and the question whether methods of contraception are permissible or not often rest on the unconscious assumption: *continually repeated, regular sexual intercourse is absolutely necessary for the maintenance of a marriage in its total aspect*. Not that I would wish to deny this presupposition —conscious or unconscious; but I certainly think that it has to be relativized. In my opinion, the most basic premiss should go like this: what is absolutely necessary to the maintenance of a Christian marriage (viewed in its totality) is *love*. This sounds like a truism, or at any rate like battering at an open door. Yet it is not so; for the traditional Catholic morality has not seen it that way.

Of course, the traditional morality has never denied that love is an indispensable norm for a good marriage. But when it came to the question of sexual intercourse, other norms were adduced: norms deriving from the "nature" of man—nature here being understood first and foremost in a biological-cum-physiological sense. If the sexual function were properly exercised—in a biological and physiological respect—and if the biological consequences were not impeded, then this sexual act was a *good* one, because it "accorded with nature". After that, it was but a short step to identifying the natural law (taken in this sense) with the divine order of law—and the circle of ethical argument was complete.

So long as sexual intercourse occurred along the right biological-cum-physiological lines, everything in the garden was lovely, so to speak, where the traditional morality was concerned. Now we would want to argue that even a biologically and physiologically commendable sexual act within a lawful marriage can be immoral. It can be immoral when it results not from genuine love but rather from self-gratification. Even sexual intercourse can be mere masturbation on one side or on both, can become a nightly routine, can be in a manner an enforced act, can be an exaction, can fail to take any account of the sexual tempo of the other party, and so forth. The person who in his or her sexual intercourse (and even when engaged in other physical endearments) puts first their own covetous self-gratification, is treating "love" as a technique for "self-release" and is laying a firm foundation for a broken marriage.

We would contend that in all the above-mentioned circumstances sexual intercourse is immoral while it is not motivated by at any rate a rudimentary form of love. In the traditional morality (aside from certain exceptions) this possibility was simply not envisaged.

Love, therefore, is necessary to the Christian marriage *in toto*; and it is also indispensable in any marriage that is to evince a quality of moral goodness. Sexuality plays an important rôle in bringing together two people, in the meeting of the sexes; it is the chief factor in engendering real love and stimulating its growth; it demands physical expression, naturally enough, in the sexual embrace; it is part of the very fabric of love, yet cannot be identified with it.

In our day there is a danger of giving undue value to sexuality and especially to the act of sex as such. The latter is *a necessary condition* for the attainment and growth of the special love between a man and a woman; but it is not in itself absolutely necessary to the complete wholeness of a marriage. The only absolute necessity is love. There are circumstances in which the sexual act cannot take place or ceases to be feasible, as, for example, during a confinement and during menstruation, in the case of protracted illness of one of the partners, or when impotence develops, and so forth. Suppose, for instance, that an illness has developed of such a nature that the sexual act can never again take place: it is not to be denied that a crisis can overtake the marriage, that the relationship may incur some damage, that in some cases the marriage will be very difficult to live with; yet we know from what happens in actual practice that it is not necessarily broken or destroyed.

So a marriage still makes sense, and is still a *genuine* marriage, even when the sexual side of it can no longer be implemented. The supreme thing about married life is not the sexual act, however persistently repeated; it is the love which inspires the act, leads up to it and flows from it.

Thus *the sexual purpose* of marriage is not reproduction or sexual relief or social security; nor is it a remedy for loneliness. But all these ends *together* take on meaning when —and only when—they are subsumed within a context and atmosphere of love.

We would do well, however, not to fall into the trap of talking about love without defining at all what we mean by it. Something more, therefore, needs to be said. "Love" is a word used in many contexts and in many different senses:

there are various "stages" or "aspects" of love, one might say. If in the early stage of sexual experience carnal desire *(eros)* is the predominant feature, this must lead on—looking at it, that is, from a Christian standpoint—to a warmth of affection and mutual sympathy (learning to "stick by" the other, recognizing his or her claims as a person in their own right, sheer comradeship), until in the end all of this comes to be imbued with Christian love *(agape)*—a love which involves the readiness to give of one's self in compassion and in sacrifice, yet also to forbear for the other's sake.

The Church as adjudicator on the question of birth-control

What then is to be the norm for the estate of matrimony, if indeed birth-control has become a practical necessity? We would reply: the norm is still love—Christian love—with that specific and peculiar quality which this love assumes within the man–woman relationship in marriage. Here, however, the difficulties begin. Does love for his wife and children require that, confronted with the need to limit the size of his family, a man resort to the use of contraceptives? (We leave aside here the possibility of the rhythm method.) Is continuing with sexual intercourse so closely bound up with the maintenance of marital affection that love can actually make it essential for preventive measures to be taken? The answer will be different in each individual case; and for the moment it is not possible to settle this issue. As a result, the suggestion is increasingly made that any decision with regard to birth-control and the use of contraceptives is in the first instance a matter for the couple concerned. But can we pronounce the use of contraceptives "a good thing", morally speaking, without more ado? We shall come back to this presently.

What we would maintain, however, is that if love does constitute the supreme norm in a marriage, it may be that in the matter of birth-control love will demand that the sex factor should take a back seat, *for the sake of that love itself*. In saying this I am not by any means contending that total abstention in such circumstances is the ideal thing; for total abstention is in itself no ethical ideal at all.

What we wish to stress is that the sexual factor must be relativized: it retains a purposive function—that is, it must continue to serve the interests of love. We have said already that to represent the sexual factor in marriage as absolutely requisite, as a basic human necessary, is to overstate the case; for then, surely, sex would be as vital a necessity as eating, drinking and breathing—which it certainly is not. If it were a biological necessity, then merely being celibate or unmarried would do violence to human nature itself.

At this juncture I may well find myself in danger of being profoundly misunderstood; and so I want to state most emphatically that in saying what I have said I do not mean to dismiss sexuality as a trivial matter (a recognized foible among clerics). Sexuality is one of those basic functions in man which underlie almost every form of association and intercourse between human beings; and it is one of those creative forces in human society, without which the world of men would grow unimaginably chill, would indeed cease even to exist.

But it is still the case that the essential function of sexuality is to serve a given end—a function which must not be repressed, but which can be sublimated to love ("sublimation" here being understood in its religious rather than its Freudian dimension). Man's sexuality is then harnessed to his need to grow towards an affective humanity which for the Christian must issue in *agape*, in Christian love.

Having thus insisted upon the primacy of love in the married state and having described sexuality in a relativizing sense as a serviceable function, we are still left with the question: are we to say that the use of contraceptives in particular cases is morally good or at least tolerable?

The moral theologians are here saddled with some awkward ecclesiastical pronouncements. Of course, there has been no *ex cathedra* statement on this question; but Pius XI prohibited the use of contraceptives in an encyclical *(Casti connubii)*. This has been the only pronouncement to be addressed to the whole Church and to be of a universal character. There have since been a number of declarations by Pius XII; but these have clearly had a particular reference, in that they were addressed to the Italian Midwives Association (1951), to the (likewise) Italian organization *Fronte della Famiglia* (1951) and to the people who took part in a couple of international congresses (1956 and 1958). Although these utterances are naturally not to be discounted, it is Pius XI's encyclical, *Casti connubii*, to which one must attach most weight. That encyclical dates, however, from 1930. We do not think it too much to say that the whole problem of birth-control appears in quite a different light now from what it did at the time of this papal pronouncement. It is noticeable how, one way and another, people are seeking to find a justification for birth-control through the use of contraceptives. Of those who have tried so far the best known are W. van der Marck, O.P., Mgr J. M. Reuss, L. Janssens and Dr John Rock.[10] All these writers set out to achieve a solution by re-interpreting the various ecclesiastical pronouncements in the light of fresh scientific evidence or by seeking, within the framework of the moral system as it now stands, to deepen and broaden existing principles. The impression one sometimes gets from these endeavours is of men of subtle, hair-splitting intelligence, all hunting for loopholes in the mesh of moral theology. Far be it from me to cast a slight on such efforts or to underestimate their value; for they spring out of a genuine pastoral involvement and concern. The article by W. van der Marck in particular shows that this moral theologian has made it his task to work his way through all the existing literature on the subject—an example, surely, of incredible courage and assiduity!

Yet all these endeavours start from the declared ecclesiastical verdict, so to speak, and from the principles of moral theology that have been built upon it. The question as I see it, however, is whether, with the new way of envisaging the Church before us, we ought not to be approaching the problem from an entirely different angle. The question is whether, in this matter of the use of contraceptives, the Church is required to give a verdict at all—at any rate in the manner in which this has been done to date. If we are really open to the current process of change in the world and in the Church-as-she-stands-within-that-world, then we must have an eye to what Robinson calls "man's coming of age": *mankind has reached its majority, has grown up*; and by this is meant not adulthood in the psychosomatic sense, but the fact that, because of scientific progress and the possibility which now exists in many quarters of thinking for oneself, man is in a position to solve many problems with the help of that same science, that thinking and the utilities which science provides. And we refer here to problems which in former times men were content to leave to the Church to resolve (to the governing circles, the hierarchy, of the Church, that is to say).

There are many areas in respect of which, in the past, the hierarchical Church claimed the exclusive right and authority to have the final say (regarding the State, for example, the sphere of secular politics). In many fields the Church has been obliged—if sometimes only after centuries of protest—to relinquish that claim; and it nearly always turned out to be for her own good when she did so.

It seems to me that many aspects of married life—and specifically the "contraception" issue—constitute what is first and foremost a human problem, a problem of mental and physical health in the public sector, which falls within the competency of doctors, psychologists, sociologists, demographers and other experts. With guidance from these scientists, grown-up Christians can far better judge for themselves whether in any given set of circumstances birth-control is necessary or not and what methods are desirable or are best suited to that end.

Accordingly, I consider birth-control to be a problem that

with the help and protection of competent scientific services people nowadays can best be left to solve for themselves. In an age when in many fields men were still incompetent and immature, it was natural for them to be asking this and that of the Church; and the Church, understanding herself to be—as indeed she is—the possessor and champion of divine truth, drew the problems laid before her into the realm of religion and answered them by appealing to principles presumed to stem from natural or supernatural revealed truths. In point of fact, this did not always work out; and in trying to make it do so the Church became too much enmeshed, perhaps, in legalities. Solutions and answers were provided —but at the level of hair-splitting argument based on the niceties of Church law and of moral casuistry.

My whole wish and endeavour, therefore, is to free Christian morality from its tendency to legalism. A new morality will have to be built upon, and in terms of, Christian love and the vital task with which it confronts us.

From legal code towards a freely informed conscience

You may well be wondering: has the Church then nothing to say on questions relating to marriage and on a matter like contraception? She has, of course; but then it really must be *the Church*—the whole Church, that is, and not just her hierarchical sector. For this Church, this new people of God, is in duty bound to set her attitude to life, and all the activities which flow from that, in the light of the Gospel, of God's message for mankind, and to examine them in that light. The new people of God is a people-on-the-move; and it is its business to be continually making sure whether it really is on the move or not. The Church must be taking stock again and again of the unlimited task laid upon us by the Gospel. The job of the hierarchical Church is to enunciate the morality intrinsic to the Gospel and thus to create a positive climate within which the Christian will understand the nature of his tasks, be able to form his conscience and act in the full light of that conscience on his own responsibility.

As new developments occur, they give rise to new ethical cruxes which the Christian must carefully consider; but then this must be a genuine consideration : that is, there must be a climate in which the hierarchy and non-hierarchical Christians can conduct their deliberations with real understanding on both sides. And as the problem involved will nearly always have to do with persons and society, no reflecting upon it should be out of touch with those human sciences that are immediately relevant to it.

From such consultation, such reasoning together, certain pointers can emerge, the function of which will be simply to help and guide the Christian in making his personal decisions of conscience. Any codified form of rules, of commands and prohibitions, will quickly become out of date and for many married couples will only prove a source of anguished fears and doubts. It will also hinder Christian people from attaining a mature and informed conscience. "The fact that individuals vary so much, that men and nations and cultures are so diversely situated, that there are so many psychological states and conditions, that the faculty men have of expressing themselves is so wide-ranging and flexible—all this must make us realize that every attempt to codify on an *a priori* basis must fail to correspond to the real state of affairs."[11]

For the Church to consider and offer counsel as to the morality of this or that attitude towards certain problems of married life can certainly help in some respects to guide and inform the Christian conscience; but that is not at all the same thing as laying down an order or a prohibition, backed by clerical authority, within the context of an ecclesiastical code of law.

I am convinced, therefore, that the matter of birth-control should be lifted out of the sphere of ecclesiastical legislation and treated primarily as a human problem of spiritual, mental and physical welfare; and then its moral implications can still be subject to investigation and questioning within the Church as a whole.[12]

Moral ambiguity and final redemption

What has caused me a certain degree of concern is the evidence that some pastoral counsellors, in their excessive eagerness to free married people from their guilt-feelings, represent the use of contraceptives as in certain cases *morally good*, without any qualification. This, as I see it, is going just too far. Now I am not saying that to use contraceptives is immoral. Between moral and immoral, black and white, there is a twilight area of actions that on the one hand are justifiable, are needful, are excusable, are in certain circumstances and in a human context sensible and right, but on the other hand cannot in themselves be classed as actions that when set in the light of the life Christians are challenged to live are thoroughly good or even perfect. Perhaps we should say that most of the things men do have this character of being morally ambiguous.

When, however, doubts do arise—and especially when people voice contradictory opinions (the use of contraceptives is mortal sin; the use of contraceptives is morally good) —then the thing is to investigate and find out, if possible, in what this moral ambiguity of a particular course of action consists. This we have already made some attempt to do. It is in any case matter for an *open discussion* in the Church, for a discussion as broadly based as we can make it. On that sort of showing the Church would be able to carry out a good deal more effectively her part in informing the conscience of people at the personal level. I would myself maintain that in the "let's sanction contraceptives with no strings attached" approach there is a concealed suggestion which fails to relativize sufficiently the sexual factor in married life.

The danger nowadays is that the sexual side of marriage be overprized as the "climax" and accorded independent status, whereas—viewed in the context of our faith—sex as an element in marital experience has to be put *to the service* of Christian love, or at any rate must become an integral part of it. Set this whole question in the perspective of Christian love, and sexuality at once begins to assume its proper and relative place; and the moral ambiguity of a thing like contraception becomes evident. Then lastly, we believe that we have here the basis for a discussion of these issues within the ecumenical dialogue.[13]

Our faith instructs us that in the end everything has value only in so far as it is "for the Kingdom of God's sake". That is the Kingdom where Christian love has triumphed and prevails. Married people must so construe and realize their love that in it they not only cleave to each other but also together cleave as a living, loving unity to the Church—to the Church and ultimately to the Kingdom of God, in which they will find their love redeemed and raised to glory.

Birth-control is a practical problem; but in our efforts to solve it we seem to have reached an impasse. We have dwelt on it at perhaps rather considerable length; yet we needed to do so if we were to show *at the practical level* how a moral problem can begin to look quite different when we base ourselves on a new vision of the Church and on a real understanding of what "catholicity" might imply in the moral sphere. We can break out of the impasse and find that fresh room is then available for a—perhaps more faithful—approach to present-day ethical problems.

VI

Catholicity and Reformation

In the next two chapters we shall try to get a better grasp of the depth-dimension of catholicity in a further aspect: namely, that which concerns our relationship with those who do not belong to the Roman Catholic Church—a relationship that should be marked by openness, dialogue and a readiness to listen and to hear. We shall have to confine ourselves to two groups: the Christians of the Reformation and the atheists of Russian Communism.

We are conscious of the fact that this is a very restricted choice. Consequently, it will do little more than illustrate what an attitude of readiness for dialogue could involve over a wider field. It is a pity that we cannot explore here the question of dialogue with the non-Christian religions.[1]

The reaction of the Church to the Reformation

Because the Catholic Church is now taking an active part in the ecumenical movement, some have been led to think that the Church is already at a deep level in dialogue with the world of the Reformation. Then something happens—like, for instance, all the hubbub and excitement caused by Princess Irene's change of Church allegiance—that serves to reveal something of the tensions and problematical aspects inherent in this dialogical relationship with the Reformation. We may suspect, therefore, that something is wrong in principle with "the Rome–Reformation parley", or at least that the basis for it is inadequate and needs somehow to be reorientated. We shall come back to this later on. It would seem to me that if we are to have a proper grasp of how things stand at present, it is desirable and useful to begin by looking at how the Church reacted towards the Reformation in the first place.

There can be no doubt about that: the Church regarded the sixteenth-century Reformation as a defection *en masse* from the Mother Church—but also as an assault on the very existence of the Church as such. Hence her reaction, which was essentially defensive: a policy of "closing the ranks" and of isolation. This made it pretty well impossible, from the very start, for her to understand what the Reformation was all about and what it was aiming at. The consequence was that from then on she became a "protected territory", a kind of "religious reserve" (Rogier). Thereafter, the Catholic Church gave up any attempt to get to grips with Protestantism and the ideas informing the Reformation—which is not to say that she did not have a reformation of her own. The Reformation did of course touch off a reforming process within the Roman Catholic Church; but this Counter-Reformation was fed not by the impulses motivating the Protestant Reformers, but by various reforming movements of the preceding period (propagandists for reform, individuals bent on reforming the religious orders, certain bishops, the revival of "high scholasticism", *devotio moderna*, mysticism). But so far as the Reformation itself was concerned, the shutters were down—as is evidenced by the fact that the reforming process within Catholicism came about outside the geographical area affected by the Reformation, that is, in Italy and Spain. The Roman Catholic Church has in large measure had a Romance or South European character ever since.[2]

The internal process of reform was slow in getting under way. It was only after the catastrophe of 1527, when Rome was sacked by the Imperial troops, that things really began to move. Pope Paul III appointed a number of able Cardinals, recognized the principal Order of the Counter-Reformation, the Jesuits, and in 1545 opened the Council of Trent. There is no denying that important things were accomplished by that Council. In the field of dogma the decrees dealt with the sources of revelation, original sin, justification, the sacraments and the sacrifice of the Mass; the disciplinary decrees dealt with marriage, the training of the clergy and the setting up of diocesan seminaries for priests, the obligation of bishops to reside, the inhibition of episcopal pluralities and of plural benefices and prebends, the proper duties of bishops and Cardinals, and so on. Reform in the exercise of various ecclesiastical offices was desperately needed; and this the disciplinary decrees had at last accomplished.

Yet this assembly of the Church showed little openness towards the real aims of the Reformation. Where doctrine was concerned, the Council of Trent set out to establish firmly what Catholic teaching was and to show wherein it differed from that of the Reformation. That is not to say that the motive spirit here was a sheer anti-Protestantism: the decrees were a successful attempt to pick a way through the controversies of the various theological schools. Also, a real effort was made to word all this doctrine in a more biblical language.

The Council did set in motion a reform within the Church. Nevertheless, the fact remains that this Catholic reforming process was very largely a direct opposition to Protestantism, a "Counter Reformation". It was essentially a bid to restore the *status quo*, and not a genuine re-forming. No one had really set out to understand, "from inside", what the Reformers were about, or to grasp and give reality to what the Protestants were quite properly seeking to renew, in order—so far as might be possible—to meet Protestantism half way, in penitence and love. On the contrary, the aim of all this internal Catholic reform was to do battle with Protestantism; and it was a plan of battle rather than a means to conciliation. The general tendency was to preserve and uphold the existing order, to look towards the past —when things were so much better—and to aim at reviving that. The practical outcome was to make catholicity inflexible and to render it stultified and repressed.

The possibility of giving to the liturgy, to the celebration of the Mass, a new form based on an understanding of the aims and insights of the Reformation was rejected; and the forms of public worship were simply "restored to their pure state", the primary model for this being *not* the liturgy as it is shown forth in the Bible and was celebrated in the Apostolic period, but the liturgical practice of the Middle Ages.

In theology too no effort was made to arrive at new forms, worked out on a biblical basis. The aim was a defensive one: "to keep doctrine pure". The same proclivity was evident in the pastoral sphere and in the government of the Church. What everywhere prevailed was a desire simply to conserve and maintain as much as possible of the traditional way of doing things. From the time of Pope Paul IV's pontificate on, a hardening process set in which strikes us now as something quite incredible. It was a period when reckless use was made of the Inquisition, while the missionary enterprise in distant continents came to grief through sheer unadaptability.

Thus minds were fast shut in an implacable hostility towards Protestantism. The not especially attractive by-products of this are sufficiently well known: negatively-toned polemics and narrowmindedness, the use of violence to stamp out errors and defects and of inquisitorial methods to maintain a doctrine "pure and undefiled"—and, finally, machination of various kinds, designed to further purely confessional interests. That all this found parallel expression in a staunchly anti-Catholic Protestantism is cold comfort for us.

There was no definitive change in this attitude to the Reformation until the pontificate of Leo XIII. He endeavoured, in a succession of encyclicals, to induce a more ecumenical temper among Catholics. He appealed for unity and discussed the basis for possible contacts with the Reformation: the common faith in Holy Scripture and love for Jesus Christ. This marked the beginning of a process which despite its ups and downs presents a stage by stage growth of ecumenical insight—a process that in 1960 reached its highest point so far in the setting up of the Secretariat for Promoting Christian Unity. It is an entirely new institution in the Church, and was established on the initiative not of the Roman Curia, but of Pope John himself. Cardinal Bea was appointed its President and Mgr J. W. Willebrands its Secretary. The General Secretary of the World Council of Churches, Dr W. A. Visser 't Hooft, exclaimed with enthusiasm: "The Church of Rome has now provided a rendezvous where Christians coming from outside are not only spoken to—the Catholic Church has been doing that for a long time—but where they themselves can speak and know that what they say is really being listened to".

This change, this growth in ecumenical temper, has been written about in considerable detail elsewhere.[3] The disposition that now prevails in many quarters within the Catholic Church could be summed up as follows: there is a receptive spirit, a readiness *to take a really open attitude towards the Reformation, towards what it stood for originally and what it stands for today.*

The snag in the ecumenical dialogue

This openness towards the Reformation and what it stands for implies a radical shift in the Catholic attitude regarding Protestantism. Now a change of attitude and mental outlook is important; but the trouble starts as soon as this *volte-face* has to be translated into action. Whenever a new prospect opens up, people are always a bit impetuous; and it is undeniable that in some quarters—more especially in Germany—some rash and foolishly amateur things were done in the ecumenical sphere. Normally, this kind of thing sorts itself out of its own accord; or else it is enough for the local Church authorities to issue a caution. It was most regrettable, therefore, that in 1948 the Holy Office stepped in with a *monitum* or admonition: the bishops were reminded that they should strictly enforce certain canons of ecclesiastical law. Their attention was drawn to canon 1325 par. 3, which lays it down that permission to take part in confessionally "mixed" theological conversations must be sought in advance from the Holy See. The *monitum* also hammered home the canons forbidding any active participation in non-Catholic church services. Many Catholics felt distress and dismay at this document, because of its purely negative intent and formal, juridical tone. As a result of the protests touched off by the *monitum*, there appeared in 1949 the "Instruction on the Ecumenical Movement". The contents of this were much more positive. Not only was due respect paid to the ecumenical concern of Catholics, but the bishops were enjoined "discreetly to further and to guide this interest". Expertly qualified priests were to be assigned to the task; and care was to be taken to ensure that non-Catholics be properly informed. What is more, the bishops were given leave for the future to permit on their own authority the holding of ecumenical conversations.[4]

The extremely cautious attitude which inspires the whole Instruction is not unconnected, perhaps, with a view traditionally held regarding the *oikoumene* and the Catholic Church—a view that we would want to designate the snag or stumbling-block in the dialogue. We refer, of course, to the idea that the Catholic Church is the one, true Church of Christ and that therefore in all dialogue with Reformed Christians the ultimate goal of the catholic *oikoumene* must involve the *return* of Protestants to the Catholic Church. If that is so, we have an unsatisfactory basis for any really ecumenical parley with the Reformation. The principle of "return to the true fold under the one chief shepherd" implies in the last analysis an isolation of the Catholic Church *vis-à-vis* the *oikoumene*. One can try to smooth over this principle, one can fight shy of it; but if it is true, there will always be an element of misgiving on the part of our Reformed brethren, because the most eirenic discussion cannot be dissociated altogether from a notion of proselytizing at some hidden level.

So what we shall need to do is to examine this principle of

a "return"—which is so deeply rooted in the Catholic tradition—and ask ourselves just what amount of truth there is in it. The first thing, though, is to express in the briefest possible terms the attempts that have so far been made to settle the principle itself. I think that these attempts to reduce the principle to its bare essentials can be brought under three heads, as follows: [5]

1. We are the one, true Church of Christ; this is an article of faith. But we have been thinking about this and have now come to realize that our Church needs to be fundamentally renewed and reformed.
2. The Roman Catholic Church is said to be "the true *oikoumene*" because we believe that God has imparted the fullness of his gifts to this Church—the fullness not only of the message but of the means of salvation. But then one must make a point of affirming that this fullness of God's gifts resides and operates in our Church insufficiently; so that our living out of the faith that is in us lacks the abundant richness willed by God.
3. The Roman Catholic Church is the one, true Church and "the true *oikoumene*"; but we recognize that God's gifts are to be found among the separated Christians and are operative in their lives. There can be no quibbling over the right of these ecclesiastical associations of Christians to be described as "Churches".

It is plain from all this how difficult it is for us to give a clear and definitive meaning, in the context of the ecumenical scene, to such terms as "one, true Church", "true *oikoumene*", or even to the principle of "return". I do not believe that the principles enunciated under those three heads will ever enable us to break out of the impasse of the dialogue with the Reformation.

The snag is that the whole approach in the three articles that we have just set down is wrong—or at any rate it calls for a drastic re-orientation. If we grant "the eventualizing character" of the Church and the fact of its being *"en route* for the *oikoumene*", then in order to come to terms with these realities on a right basis we must learn to think in a historical and existential way. In Catholic thought this kind of approach is still relatively novel. That is why we come across quite a number of theologians who fully intend to go to work on historical and existential lines, but are constrained by the force of tradition and of the training they have received to relapse, almost unnoticeably, into a mode of essentialist, dogmatic thinking which is an indifferent version of its kind, anyway.

What are these essentialist-dogmatic concepts? They are: that the Roman Catholic Church already *is* the one, true Church and already is "the *oikoumene*", that God *has* imparted his gifts to the Roman Catholic Church in their *fullness*. Concepts of an existential-historical character are: that the Roman Catholic Church "has to be fundamentally renewed and reformed", that the *oikoumene* expresses an aspect of our Church, that the full range of God's gifts resides also with the other Churches, that a distinction must be made between the Roman Catholic Church as she has evolved in history and "the ideal Catholic Church".

In point of fact, these two ways of thinking and of looking at things often clash head on; and therefore whatever conclusion is finally arrived at is bound to be unsatisfactory. Sometimes, indeed, it is merely confusing. Consequently, if we are going to think and talk about "the *oikoumene*", we must adopt—and consistently maintain—a new approach. In what follows I intend to do precisely that. I have no thought at all of laying down the last word on the subject here. Heaven forbid! It will be just a tentative effort to shed a little more light on a matter which is of such extreme importance to us all.

A new approach to the ecumenical problem

The "return" principle is usually enunciated in two traditional formulas: a "return to the true fold of Christ under the one, chief shepherd" and "return to the Father's house". These formulas are so familiar to us that we scarcely notice how a particular interpretation of two Gospel parables is here being applied to the situation of a divided Christendom. Obviously, the parables in question are those of the Good Shepherd (John 10. 11–18) and of the Prodigal Son (Luke 15. 11–32).[6]

Now it is always dangerous to apply Gospel sayings to concrete, historical events. When we do this, the Word of God is not being expounded or declared. Rather are we rummaging in the Gospel for a justification of some course of action in history, a piece of behaviour or an attitude. Applying these two parables to the rift with the Reformation is justifiable neither as exegesis nor as hermeneutics. To identify the sheepfold and the Father's house with the Catholic Church—and the sheep who are not of the fold, as well as the Prodigal Son, with Protestantism—is *simpliste* and loveless withal. In the parable of the Good Shepherd Jesus would have us understand that he is the Messiah—the Shepherd of Ezekiel 34. 11—appointed by God. "Who are not of this fold" means: "not belonging to the chosen people of the Jews"—in other words, the heathen who are to be brought into the flock that is led by Jesus. In the parable of the Prodigal Son the point being made is that the father's tenderness and compassion mirror the goodness and mercy of God; and the Elder Son's behaviour reflects the disposition of the Jewish people. Let it be noticed that the parallel suggested by the "return" interpretation ceases to work at this point; for the Elder Son of the story would then be the Catholics. They have, after all, remained in the "Father's house" of the Catholic Church, have they not? The notion that the Gospel formulas can be construed to support the "return motif" is, as we can now see, untenable. If we want to maintain that motif at all, and at the same time show even a spark of ecumenical concern, we must at any rate stop couching it in a terminology derived from the Gospels.

Without getting ourselves too much involved with the "return principle" formulas, let us now start looking for the new approach by which the impediment to the dialogue with the Reformation may be removed. To do this we shall have to pick up again some of the ideas propounded in the first chapter on the Church as a "task" and a "happening". We pointed out there that the Church is not a realized and finished entity but an event-in-process that fulfils itself in history (as well as through people). The Church, as the calling together of men under a single Head, is not a cut-and-dried *thing*, given us by God, but a continuing *task* and charge, laid upon all who own allegiance to her. So also unity, catholicity and ecumenicity are given by Christ to his Church not as so many assets but as a *commission*, not as a gift but as a *task*. The Church has not summoned together all men into unity in Christ already: only *in principle*—that is, "as a beginning"—she is that unification of all. Here then lies also the meaning of the term "catholic" and of what is so closely akin to it, *oikoumene*: universal, forming together a single whole, all-embracing.

In the course of her history the Roman Catholic Church has certainly understood this commission and this task—to bring all men into unity in Christ—but she has not always put them into effect in her conduct. The missionary *élan* of the early Christian centuries is something that we cannot enjoin today; nor indeed are the methods which it prompted to be entirely recommended. But it was born of the longing to make this Christian oneness a reality; and it sprang from a profound awareness that the catholicity of the Church was a "strict order" and that Christians were not to let it slide. That evangelizing fervour and sense of mission in the early Church first began to decrease at the time of the struggle between Rome and Constantinople and then, after the Reformation, fell away. Admittedly, there did ensue a period of intense missionary activity beyond the borders of Europe; but in Western society there grew up within the Church that defensive attitude so often referred to already—an attitude centred more and more on protecting and conserving the group as it was.

Unity was looked for then in a "unity of forms" (a uniform language, uniform liturgy, uniform theology), accompanied by the centralizing of the Church's administration in Rome. All this is understandable enough, as a reaction; but it is in fact a substitute for that unity, and only served to obscure and undermine the fullness of catholicity. The ecumenical movement has made us acutely aware once more of what it means for the Church of Christ to be under obligation to be catholic, to be an *oikoumene* and to be *one*. Part and parcel of the Roman Catholic's creed is his belief in the one, holy, catholic and apostolic Church: that is, a belief in the Church of Christ. The Catholic is justified in recognizing that Church of Christ in the Roman Catholic Church as a historic growth, and thus in owning allegiance to that Church; but he. is not justified in thinking that in the Roman Catholic Church he *possesses* catholicity, ecumenicity and unity in all their fullness. Unity and catholicity reside in the Roman Catholic Church as a challenge to be met and as a charge upon her. What, then, does "the *oikoumene*" imply? It implies not only renewal and re-adjustment in the Church but, first and foremost, *conversion*—a conversion in the biblical sense of the word *(metanoia)*: conversion *from* all the sins and all the guilt (accruing from history) that stand in the way of the unity of men in Christ—such as the unforthcoming attitude in face of "the others", the mistrust, the propensity to being an institutionalized power-group, the complacency, the rationalism in theology and legalism in the moral sphere, the self-esteem that ecclesiastical office sometimes brings, the tendency to treat the layman as less than adult and the shortcomings in ministration of the Word. Perhaps it would be more correct to say, therefore, that the *oikoumene* stands or falls not by a return of the Protestants to the Roman Catholic Church but by a return of that Church to a thorough, all-round expediting of her original commission and task.

The oikoumene *as a task*

Such a return was, after all, the aim of the sixteenth-century Reformers: not to found a new Church but to reform the Church, which had grown—and gone awry—through the course of her history, in accordance with the pristine purity of the mandate given in the Gospel. It was partly our fault that this strong impulse to bring about reform died away in the end through the incomprehension and inflexibility of a Church governed too much by political considerations and too much conformed to this world. That is why the process of reform was bound to lead to a divided Christendom. Pope Paul VI was right to make a confession of guilt during the Council. This *Mea culpa* had only one possible implication. It meant that a new course had been set: towards a real, ready-for-action *openness with respect to the true aims and purposes of the Reformation.*

How then do the Roman Catholic Church and the other Christian Churches stand towards each other as regards the *oikoumene?* Neither the Roman Catholic Church nor the various Protestant Churches can describe themselves at present as the true *oikoumene* in all its fullness. We are all entitled, of course, to see ourselves as *on the way* towards it.

The individual may see the ecumenical task as being effectuated better in one particular Church, or at any rate may conclude that the task has more chance of being effectuated in that particular Church than in another one. He can show preference, therefore, for this or that particular Church. The Roman Catholic will firmly believe that the ecumenical task is being accomplished by his Church, because he recognizes in that Church the primitive structure of the ministry of the Apostles with Peter at the centre, and the continuity of this throughout the centuries intervening. He believes, furthermore, that this historic continuity rests on an ecclesial identity with the Petrine-apostolic Church of the first Pentecost. He knows from experience that in his

Church the Gospel continues to be proclaimed and the sacraments administered in accordance with this Gospel.

But he knows too that his Church has to undergo a conversion, in so far as the administrative and governing authority in the Church, instead of serving the ends of teaching and preaching the Gospel, has all too often seen itself as a *power* exerting authority over the minds and consciences of immature people; a conversion also from the superfluous eccelesiastical trimmings that are part of the legacy of history and somehow have been given an absolute status, although they do not belong to the essence of Christianity; a conversion that will even have to entail the relativizing of certain theological conclusions which in some dogmas have been put too much on the same level of absolute truth with the Gospel message itself; a conversion from the great deficiencies in the proclamation of the Word which have led to a one-sided emphasis on the sacraments and given rise to the designation "Church of sacraments"; conversion too from certain forms which have accrued to ecclesial offices, especially to the Petrine office: it could be that for the Protestant what stands in the way of belief in the Petrine office—which *is* based on the Bible—is the *form* which that office currently assumes.

The Reformed Christian will believe in his Church's fitness to accomplish the ecumenical task, because he considers that that Church best preserves the purity of the Gospel. But he too must be persuaded that his Church has still to undergo a *metanoia*, if the *oikoumene* is to become a reality. The "protest" of the Reformation was in the nature of a reaction; and that in itself imposed a one-sided character on the process of reform—a one-sidedness that could well stand in the way of a pure and unalloyed proclamation of the Gospel. In the last few decades people have begun to realize that the sacramental character of the Church and her worship has been soft-pedalled out of a certain fear of "Catholicizing tendencies". Must it not be asked whether the fact that the Reformation abhorred the idea of ecclesiastical office as a power-wielding institution has not produced notions of it which amount to caricature? Ought not the traditional arguments brought against the Petrine office to be re-evaluated; and is there really no place at all in the Reformation for such a thing as a Petrine office?

These are not questions calculated in a covert and round-about way to hint at a "return" of any sort. They are questions which I think that I may be allowed to put, simply on the basis of our common stake in the Bible. Furthermore, I believe that one of the key issues keeping us apart is the way in which we envisage the *officium* (and consequently, the Church). I am convinced that thorough investigation will in the end show that on many points of dogma no profoundly essential difference exists—only a difference of accent and emphasis. I have been led to think this by my experience of many ecumenical discussions—but also by Hans Küng's book on Karl Barth's doctrine of *Justification*. (Küng shows that this doctrine in Barth is not essentially different from the doctrine as agreed at the Council of Trent.) Hence my questions regarding *officium* and Church.

These questions are in no way meant to indicate what the terms of a "conversion" on the Reformed side would have to be. That would be improper and arrogant on my part. I have only been trying to point to the need for us both to be persistently asking ourselves what it is that Christ expects of us, what the charge that he lays upon us involves.

A basis for dialogue with the Reformation

Under this head I would like to list a number of points which we might all consider as a basis for an ecumenical dialogue:

1. Above all else, there is our belief that Christ has willed our unity. That being so, we must also believe that that unity is not something utopian—otherwise we would no longer believe in the force of Christ's prayer for unity (John 17.

20). The prayer implies a commission that is compelling and is always with us.

2. We have to proceed from whatever it is that already makes us one *now*: namely, that in the power of one and the same Spirit, *through baptism*, we are become one single body and that we have all been made "to drink of one Spirit" (I Cor. 12, 13); we have to proceed from the Gospel which we possess in common as the Word of God (even though we may differ in our interpretation of it).

What binds us together is at a deeper level than what keeps us separated; and at that deeper level we encounter each other in the one Holy Spirit, who brings us all to acknowledge the one Lord and so affords us fellowship with the one Father. The quarrels lying at the source of our separation and the centuries of estrangement that followed have served to fix our attention only on the points of difference between us. Without denying the seriousness of our disagreements, we have grown irresistibly more and more aware of the things that we have in common.[7]

3. We have to remove all the unnecessary barriers that history has created, by a steady improvement of communication and exchange of information: not only to talk and think ecumenically but also to act ecumenically, whenever this or that new insight has been achieved. For the Catholic this means finally abandoning his "sheepfold theology" and discarding the notion that in the end unity will consist in a "return" of the Reformation to the Catholic Church in her present guise. That reciprocal communication is of the utmost urgency is not merely something suggested by the unhappy events connected with the Princess Irène's change of allegiance; the same requirement is brought home to us whenever we read summaries, from the Protestant side, of what passes for "Catholic doctrine".[8] We suspect that the need is as imperative in the other direction. Centuries of alienation have generated an imposing number of fables about the doctrine and deportment of "the other lot". These fabrications and half truths have an obstinate way of

persisting which constitutes a serious handicap for the *oikoumene*.

4. As unity does not consist in a "return", it is important that on both sides we begin, however modestly, to try and understand what "the way of the *oikoumene*" is. It is essential, therefore, that we pray *together* to the Spirit of our Lord that He will give light to us both, that we may discover that way which we can travel *together*, and which will lead us together to the one Lord Jesus and to the one Church that he has willed.

The ecumenical movement, therefore, is not a pastime for certain individuals, which one can indulge in or not, as one pleases. It is a movement in which we have to recognize the compelling influences of the Spirit. That is what Pope John did when he exclaimed: "Through east and west there stirs a wind, as it were born of the spirit, arousing attention and hope among those who are adorned with the name of Christians."[9]

If ever we spoke about the need for unity, this was in the belief that Christ has willed that unity; but in our day a compelling external necessity has been added. We Christians have a shared responsibility towards the non-Christian world, towards the other religions and towards a sceptical humanism and Communism. For that reason too we must hope that the unity which, sacramentally, we already possess in baptism may be extended, so that we are united at the Lord's table, in the communion of the one bread and the one cup.

Christ did not simply pray for this unity. He also suffered for it. For he *gave himself up* that he might consecrate his Church and make her his one Bride, without spot or wrinkle or defect, that she might be holy and without blemish (Eph. 5. 25–27).

VII

Church and Communism

Possibilities of dialogue

> *That very widespread habit of presenting things as though Christianity were simply and without remainder opposed to the Communist ordering of society . . . is extremely dangerous.*
>
> Professor Albert Dondeyne.[1]

I. Introduction

During the last hundred years Communism has been officially anathematized no less than thirteen times;[2] and nobody knows how many *ad hoc*, local condemnations have been voiced, in addition, by the Church authorities. As early as in 1846 Pius IX declared that Communism contravenes the natural law about as much as anything can *(maxime iuri naturali adversa)*; and Leo XIII called Communism "a mortal plague" *(lethiferam pestem)*. Pius XI, whose condemnations were the most numerous, says that Communism is full of errors and sophisms and in conflict with reason and divine revelation. It is bad through and through; and there is no sphere whatever in which it is permissible to co-operate with it or countenance it.[3]

Against the background of these condemnatory pronouncements it would appear that any form of dialogue with Communism is unwarranted and perilous. This conclusion is reinforced by a whole range of "self-evident facts" entrenched within the collective consciousness of Catholics. Communism, then, came to be regarded as without doubt or dispute the biggest enemy of the Church and of Christianity. Equally self-evident was the fact that Christianity and the atheistic ideology of Communism are two irreconcilable standpoints. What we were told about the conduct of the Communist rulers confirmed yet again the obviously objectionable, nay, damnable character of a political system that destroyed all who opposed it by means of persecutions, executions, acts of atrocity, arrest and imprisonment, brainwashing and the like. It seemed evident, therefore, that for the Catholic Church to engage in discussion with Communism would be quite absurd. People even went so far as to identify Communism with anti-Christ and the devil—those ancient symbols of the arch-enemies of Christianity! Thus, for example, the Director of the *Oostpriesterhulp* described discussion with Communism as "a pact with the devil".[4]

"Self-evident facts" are often dangerous, however. They are, as it were, the axioms of people's ordinary, run-of-the-mill thinking—propositions which are *so* evident that nobody thinks of questioning them.

It is not until one puts a question-mark against the said propositions that they begin to be troublesome. If we use the expression "self-evident facts" in this connection, this does not mean that the ecclesiastical documents offered no arguments for condemning Communism. We mean only that the mental outlook of the Church and of Catholics in general was firmly wedded to the idea of the total perfidy of Communism, with or without an extensive backing of argument.

During recent years, however, there has been a change in this outlook; and for the first time we hear tell of a possible dialogue with Communism.[5] This alteration has so far found a response only among a limited circle; for the thought of a possible dialogue meets with fierce resistance, even from an academic quarter.[6]

What follows, therefore, is meant to be an attempt to indicate some of the problematical aspects of the current evidences regarding Communism and at the same time to explain from what standpoint a dialogue with Communism is possible, not to say necessary.

II. The Problematical Aspects of the Conflict between Christianity and Communism

Current views regarding Communism have been formed, perhaps, too much on the basis of the godless, anti-Church and savage aspect that Communism has presented to the West. The West has let itself be too much governed by its immediate feelings of sympathy with the victims of Communism—a sympathy mixed, understandably enough, with abhorrence and disgust at an inhuman political system. The irksome reality of what Communism was in practice was always obtruding itself; and so it became wellnigh impossible to stand aloof and take a detached view. To arrive at a reconstruction of the origin and causes of Communism in the world-process as a whole which would be as objective as possible was therefore extremely difficult.

When as Christians we concern ourselves with the conflict between Christianity and Communism, we are in all honesty bound to view that conflict *in its total aspect*—which is to say that we have to locate it within the history of the Church and Christianity during the last century. If we are candid in our consideration of past events, we shall have to admit that because nineteenth-century Catholicism was so isolated and withdrawn (as were also the main Protestant denominations) and because Christianity remained so aloof from the great issues agitating the world at that time, Christianity in general—and when we say "in general", we allow that there were indeed remarkable exceptions—passed by the human misery which, among other things, resulted from the capitalist system and attended the Industrial Revolution.

Social blindness

As a consequence of economic stagnation in the seventeenth century, of the Napoleonic Wars and of the continued existence of an outdated feudal system, there arose in most countries of Europe during the last century an impoverished but ever-growing proletariat. When on top of that we have the rise of industry and the introduction within it of the capitalist economy, this already long entrenched penury—until then accepted as one of the facts of life in society—becomes a problem. The distress was no longer something that the customary forms of charity could alleviate. In some countries the property-less proletariat amounted to a fifth—in a few even to wellnigh a third—of the population. In certain countries the feudal system of large-scale landowning was the main reason for big sections of the population being impoverished. Later on, this proletariat in Western Europe was for a considerable part caught up in a rapidly expanding industrialization, which reduced the majority to a condition of still greater insecurity.

Owing to undernourishment on what came to be recognized as the normal European hunger-diet of potatoes and gin, the workers were stunted and enfeebled; while through hunger, tuberculosis and, above all, their long hours of factory work the children were even worse off.

The nineteenth century confronts us with a social and economic system that for the greater part of mankind offered little or no scope or prospect. Many children were brought into the world only to be threatened with almost immediate extinction. In England especially—where industrialization set in first—the figures tell a sad story. In Liverpool in 1840 the average expectation of life among the higher classes was thirty-five years, and among manual labourers and day-labourers fifteen years. In the County of Rutland, round about 1830, some twenty-eight per cent of the population died before they were five years old; in Essex it was thirty-one per cent, in the factory town of Preston forty-nine per cent, and in Leeds as much as fifty-two per cent. Speaking in the House of Commons in 1863, Ferrand stated that the cotton industry had then been going for ninety years, and in the course of three generations in England as a whole *nine generations* of cotton workers had been swallowed up.[7] Only if one belonged to a certain privileged class did one escape the inhuman threat posed by the socio-economic structure.

What did Christianity and the Christian Churches do in this situation? Here and there the voice of protest was heard.[8] Charitable institutions were spurred on to even greater activity. Natural law was invoked to prove that the existence of master and serf, rich and poor, was prescribed by nature[9] and that the labouring classes must rest content with their lot. In an issue of the Dutch periodical *De Katholiek* for 1880, for instance, we read that "the social question springs from a political conspiracy. The solution to the prevailing unrest lies in *contentedness*, the contented spirit with which the working people must bear their lot, because they are Christians. The last word on the social question is the kindly disposition of the better sort of persons and the charity which their love disposes them to exercise."[10]

If we now turn to what Karl Marx has to say, we get an exact description of this so-called Christian attitude. In 1847 he writes:

> *The social principles of Christianity proclaim the necessity for a ruling class and a subject class; and for the latter it merely entertains the pious wish that the former may exercise beneficence towards them. The social principles of Christianity declare that heaven is the place where all injustices will be duly rectified; and therefore these principles justify the continuation of such injustices on earth. The social principles of Christianity explain every outrage perpetrated by the oppressors on the oppressed either as a rightful punishment for original sin, or something of that sort, or as trials visited by the Lord in his infinite wisdom upon his redeemed. The social principles of Christianity encourage dullness, lack of self-respect, submissiveness, self-abasement, in short, all the characteristics of the proletariat.*[11]

What we really end up with here is a confrontation of nineteenth-century Christianity and Marxism. Over against the feeble, prevaricating attitude of Christianity towards the great human problem of the time—over against that attitude which rested satisfied with a certain amount of superficial papering over of the cracks—stands the figure of Marx as the thinker who through a piercing analysis of the real condition of society made the discovery that only a radical break-up of the socio-economic structure could put an end to the miseries of the proletariat. Marx applied himself to working out a programme that would abolish this inhumane social and economic constellation. The misery was only too real; and his programme, forged under the stress of it, is so radical that it falls into another extreme of inhumanity by seeking to eliminate everything and everybody standing in the way of a "new world". This, however, does not altogether preclude there being major positive values in Marxism to which the Christianity of the nineteenth century ought to have been open and to which Christianity must all the while remain receptive today.

There is no getting round it: the Church's isolation gave rise to a grave form of social blindness; and so it was Marx who fathered "social thinking". This is based on the idea that every person in a society has a right to certain minimal opportunities of existence, that an economic and social order must be created that will be worthy of mankind—and thus a world which matches up to the material and mental aspirations of men.

So then, this "social idea" was not the inspiration of a Christian thinker but of the atheistic philosopher Marx (and of a few others with him). It was *not* originally the Christian Churches that broke through with this social idea, but a non-Christian movement: namely, Socialism-Communism. It was not at that time the Christian Churches that rose up in defence of the most elementary rights of man, but rather the Marxists, Socialists and Communists.

The Churches, on the contrary—and their ministers too—as often as not took the side of the capitalists, of the established order that tolerated the inhumanity as part of the structure of its society. Of the Catholic Church of the nineteenth century it may be said that it was a Church so out of touch as to have lost all feeling for the mental outlook and temper of the age. Now a Church that in its thinking is not attuned to the fundamental questions of a given moment in history has lost contact with life and is no longer in a position to cope with a social crisis. In the mid-nineteenth century—just when it was most urgently needed, in fact—no Catholic socio-political programme had been evolved—let alone a doctrine of property or a Catholic doctrine of labour that would have shown the concept—one so central to the time—in a Christian light. Her closed outlook plunged the Church into a structure-crisis from which it was hard for her to extricate herself. On the heels of the French Revolution came the Restoration, eager to welcome the proffered alliance with the Church. This drove the Church, practically speaking, into the arms of the *bourgeoisie*; and that proved to be the start of a process which alienated the Church from the working class.

Of course, the "social idea" and way of thinking were not wholly absent from the Church; but at the start they were represented only by a few individuals, who often had to wage a heroic fight against a tide of misunderstanding and evil insinuations.

When we look at the climate prevailing in the Rome of the mid-century, it is evident that the social injustice that was rife in the world made little enough impact there. The Church's governing circles at that time saw her as "a religious reserve" (Rogier) or sanctuary amid a world full of errors. Her task was simply to keep the flock together, to shelter and protect it, to signalize the errors and condemn them. In his *Syllabus errorum*—a list of eighty errors, appended to the encyclical *Quanta cura* of 1864—Pope Pius IX took an uncompromising attitude: he roundly condemned all theories and movements not hallowed by centuries-old tradition. Rejected out of hand were: pantheism, naturalism and rationalism; while Socialism, Communism and secret societies, Bible Societies and associations of liberal-minded clergy were condemned in a single paragraph. The last error to be censured was the idea that "the pope of Rome could and should arrive at a conciliation and agreement with progress, liberalism and modern culture".

The Church in her directive capacity here reached the nadir of her self-isolation. That behind the Communist and Socialist movements there lay a world of social injustice and human misery had so far gone quite unnoticed. Pius IX's successor was Leo XIII. No sooner had he succeeded to the papal chair in 1878 than he condemned Socialism on theological grounds in the encyclical *Quod apostolici muneris*. In after years, however, through contact with the real situation and with non-Catholic thought, this pope grew to be more open-minded.

Thus there did at last appear the first encyclical to deal with the social issue: *Rerum novarum*. The year was 1891—just forty-three years after the Communist Manifesto. Even so, almost two decades of the twentieth century were to elapse before the ideas expressed in this encyclical had any real effect on Catholic social action.

In a retrospective attempt to create the myth of a Catholic social movement, *Rerum novarum* was strongly idealized, in order to endow Catholic social thought and action with a history reaching far back into the nineteenth century. In fact *Rerum novarum* had had little influence, either when it appeared or in the period immediately after. Furthermore, this encyclical did not aim at social *reform* but was rather an attempt at accommodation within the capitalist social and economic order. The intention was to maintain labour relations on the existing basis of a "two class" society and at the same time to improve wage-rates among the workers.[12] It is only with the encyclical *Mater et Magistra* (1961) that the basic concepts taken over from capitalism—ownership, capital and wage-agreement—are called in question and relativized for the first time.

Now I do not wish to do less than justice to the very great

deal of good that has come as a result of Catholic social doctrine; but honesty compels us to recognize that social thought and action in the Church got going too late and too slowly. Unhappily, they have been governed by a spirit of cautious compromise and have left little scope, generally speaking, for a more radical Christian humanism.

We should not be allowed *now*, therefore, to forget that Marxism and also Communism in its later Marxist–Leninist form were (and still are) a terrible indictment of a "churchified", remote, middle-class, *laisser-faire* Christianity. When we turn our thoughts to the question of a dialogue with Communism, we must be fully aware of our compromising record; and when in the conversation it becomes our turn to speak, we shall then do so with all the more diffidence and consciousness of guilt.

"Applied religion" and the established order

Atheistic Communism is an imputation of guilt laid at the door of a desiccated, saltless Christianity, riddled with ecclesiasticism. The fact is that in many parts of Europe Christianity during the eighteenth and nineteenth centuries had undergone a fatal curtailment and constriction, so far as its living expression was concerned. Religion had become a "private affair". Permeated with a drawing-room atmosphere, the practice of the faith was nearly always relegated to a man's closet or confined within the walls of some sacred edifice. Christian witness played no active and effective rôle in public life. The aristocracy, imbued with free-thinking notions, and the so-called higher classes made a point of keeping religion and the life of society in separate compartments, and saw to it that most of the clergy remained sufficiently in leading-strings to serve their own turn.

The Christianity of our grandparents and great-grandparents was infused with a mystical *Weltflucht* (a "fleeing from the world"), a strong *Jenseitigkeitserlebung* (cultivation of other-worldliness), that refused to contemplate in any way the injunction to build here and now a world in which *all* people might find it good to live. The Catholic community was like a fortress within which the faithful clung hard—and in some trepidation—to the apron-strings of Mother Church. The clergy in Russia and in most of what are now the satellite countries (especially Czechoslovakia and Hungary) for the greater part took their stand on the side of the feudal overlords and big landowners (if they did not themselves belong to that class, anyway)—and thus on the side of the very class that occasioned the misery of so many thousands.

By way of illustration, here is an outline of the situation as it was in Hungary. Prior to the Second World War, not only were sixty-seven per cent of the population Catholic, but the Catholic Church was also the principal landowner in the country. The bishops (with the Cardinal Primate at their head) were at that time still in possession of the vast territories which St Stephen, first king of the Hungarians, and his successors had given to the prelates of their period: a gift in kind, which should have enabled the Church to discharge her religious and cultural avocation without undue embarrassment or difficulty. What had seemed natural enough in the past, however, in the twentieth century had become a source of scandal and vexation among the faithful, who gradually began to ask themselves why the Catholic Church did not give up—in part, at any rate—her right to possess so much land. There were two and a half million peasants living in the bitterest poverty, because there was no land available for them. It was expected of the Church that of her own initiative she would carry through an agrarian reform, that she would surrender her position as a feudal power, the better to fulfil her spiritual mission. But *no member* of the ecclesiastical hierarchy did anything to deliver the Church from the clutches of this ancient feudal structure. Only the Cistercians—and then not until 1943—distributed five thousand hectares among the poverty-stricken peasants on their estates. When at last the Russians came, agrarian reform was put through, by main force, within a matter of days.[13]

In Russia and in various other countries social and economic wrongs were for centuries inflicted not only by the aristocracy but by the clergy too. These malpractices, built into the structure of feudalism, were not actually written into the legal codes of the countries concerned; but years of exploitation, the fact that whole sections of the population were without legal rights or status, and sheer human wretchedness at length aroused the people's sense of justice in the face of these social and economic wrongs. When the Communist revolution came and the relationships preserved by the old legal system were abrogated, the new sense of what was right and just took a course that was, to begin with, quite uncontrolled. The profiteers of the old order were massacred in their thousands; and others received long terms of imprisonment. That many innocent persons fell victim to this orgy of hatred and that the actual punishment administered was often arbitrary and atrocious must invariably appal us; yet such things belong to the nature of a revolution, when feelings of hate, pent up for centuries, are released with the force of an explosion.

During and after the Communist revolution all who had been in any way concerned with the old régime were the objects of hatred and of an urge to destroy. Because the Christian Churches almost everywhere had compromised with that régime or had been a part of it, the urge to hate and to kill was turned upon them also . . . and, albeit to a lesser extent, is turned upon Christians still.

In the light of history the problem of the conflict between Christianity and Communism appears in its true perspective. It would seem that the Catholic Church also has a mirky record; and it is a *sine qua non* that we should be aware of that, before we start thinking and talking about the potentialities of the dialogue. We Christians may identify Communism with the devil; but what if this particular devil has been conjured up *by the errors and shortcomings of Christianity itself?*

III. The Feasibility of the Dialogue

In the article by Professor B. Delfgaauw to which I have already referred[14] we find summarized a number of insuperable objections to a dialogue with Communism. The professor declares that any *rapprochement* is out of the question: (1) because Communism is too dogmatic, (2) because within the Communist world the expression of opinion is subject to censorship, (3) because Communism aims at worldwide domination and (4) because force counts for more than freedom.

Professor Delfgauw very properly relativizes these objections. It occurs to me, however, that unless her self-knowledge is extremely defective the Catholic Church cannot easily maintain objections of this sort. A frank scrutiny of her history must surely reveal that she has herself suffered under more or less the evils enumerated (and perhaps does so still). We shall leave these objections on one side, therefore, and turn our thoughts to the possibilities offered by a dialogue with Communism.

Some people immediately think of such a dialogue in terms of a "round table conference" or a discussion group. However, when we speak here of a "dialogue", we mean a "colloquy" in a wider sense. A dialogue is primarily a "game" or round of listening and speaking, in which two parties are prepared to open themselves to a *logos*—the truth-revealing word—and in that way to arrive at a joint understanding and consequently to an understanding of each other. It is assumed that each party will approach the other on a footing of equality and mutual trust. A dialogue in which the one party sets itself *a priori* above the other or insists on delimiting the themes to be pursued is naturally doomed to failure.

The points which now follow are intended to indicate the ways in which this dialogue would be feasible.

Readiness to listen

The Catholic Church has already had a good deal to say about and against Communism; but it has not done nearly the same amount of listening. In my view, what such "listening" involves in the first instance is a ready sense of the conflict between Christianity and Communism as it presents itself to us in history viewed as a whole. We have had a rough shot at achieving this in an earlier part of the chapter; and in so doing we made the discovery that Communism passes a very real judgment on our Christian society. It is in the first place a judgment regarding a specific social and economic system with which the Christianity of the Churches has identified itself or has at least compromised. Next, it is a judgment passed on a middle-class, world-denying Christianity that neglected its duty towards humanity on this earth; and finally, it is a judgment given against the Christians' conception of their God—for they had cut God down to size, so as to make him the servant of a kind of Christian party interest.

All of this should lead us, perhaps, to declare our suspicion that Communism is not so much an assault on the Message of the Gospel as on *what we have made of that message*.

Again, our "listening" will make us alive to the positive values in Communism. We shall have to try and discover what that sense of values is which inspires the voice of Communism today. I say "discover" here, because in the past we have all too easily either denied that Communism is sensible of any values or insisted that there could be "nothing in it" of positive worth, anyhow, so far as Christianity is concerned. What Catholicism has to proclaim exerts little hold over the contemporary world, because Catholicism presupposes too great a degree of perfection in its own camp and so has no eye to that world's sensibilities and to the moral values that go with them. The Catholic Church must not only preach to its own constituency but proclaim the message of Christ to the world. She cannot address herself to Communism, unless she knows what are the values of that system and acknowledges them.[15]

A start is being made with all this, as can now be seen from the "Copernican revolution" in Vatican diplomacy and from the generally new attitude to Communism. An obvious token of this was the sympathetic reception accorded to Mr Adzhubei, editor-in-chief (at that time) of *Izvestia* and son-in-law to Mr Khrushchev, by Pope John XXIII. Church authorities and diplomats conduct negotiations with Communist government officials. These new contacts at a diplomatic level and the change of tactics that they reveal are no doubt the initial outcome of the extensive information supplied to the Vatican by the sixty bishops from behind the Iron Curtain who have been attending the Council. It is regrettable, perhaps, that these negotiations have so far been pursued too exclusively with an eye to an amnesty for imprisoned priests and bishops and to restoring a certain hierarchical-canonical *status quo ante*. But in themselves the contacts made are still of value in that they offer the possibility of discussion at a deeper level.

An historical-cum-existential approach

Communism is not an ossified system, but is continuously on the move—a fact which has become more evident over the last ten years. In a recent article[16] Professor W. Banning has rightly cautioned us against the current *dogmatic* and fixed position with regard to (Russian) Communism; and he pleads for a historical approach, based on the living and shifting reality. For Communism is going through a process of profound change in many respects; and this we must know and comprehend before we can reach a judgment. There is an internal process afoot that arises out of the immanent logic of an advancing industrialization and the social, intellectual and cultural development of whole sections of the population. Of course, we can say that the totalitarianism and the dictatorship are still there. But a new generation of industrial managers, intellectuals and artists have learnt how to find ways of resolving the tensions with the régime, as and when these occur, in a sound and sensible fashion.

Not so very long ago Mr Khrushchev was making a point of the fact that Marxism is not a fixed and settled dogma but a method which in every period of history has to be applied to changing circumstances. "It is not enough," he said, "to reach for the book and look up what Lenin said. *We must think for ourselves,* study life assiduously and analyse the prevailing constellations."[17]

It is heartening to be able to record that Pope John XXIII was likewise most emphatic in urging a historical–existential approach to Communism. In the encyclical *Pacem in terris* the pope argued for making *a distinction between the false philosophical theory and the historical movement that has arisen out of it* and can be considerably affected by the changing circumstances of life. With this the pope combined a clear suggestion pointing in the direction of a dialogue: "It may be, therefore, that *positive encounters* at the practical level, which until now have looked to be inopportune or fruitless, now offer real advantages or bid fair to do so in the future." This new approach is related to the actual distribution of power in the nuclear era, which could very well be exploited in favour of a dialogue. That is why the next section is entitled:

Reaching an understanding—an indispensable need[18]

Even allowing that the Communist is fundamentally intolerant, still tolerance is wrung from him by the actual course of history, which as a matter of sheer fact has led to the "balance of power" situation. At bottom the Communist may not see the West as a serious partner for a discussion; but dialogue is forced upon him by the dilemma of peace or annihilation. Those who are opposed to dialogue are right enough when they point to the doctrine of Marx and Lenin as the ground of the present religious persecution and oppression; but then they fail to reckon sufficiently with the changes that are taking place in the world and in Communism today, the importance of which it is hard to overestimate.

The question of a dialogue must be examined not only in the light of a past phase of Communism but also from the standpoint of the future; and here we refer to the prospect being opened up by the course events are taking now. The situation today offers these possibilities: (1) atomic war—which implies, however, total annihilation; (2) unilateral disarmament—which would upset the balance of power, the very thing that constitutes the basis of the enforced tolerance; (3) maintenance of the *status quo*—but to go on living under the threat of atomic war is risky in the extreme. There remains only one further possibility: to accept the unavoidable and reach an understanding. This would involve going all out, in future, to turn the so far negative point of departure which we share into a positive kind of co-operation. "Self-interest and the instinct for self-preservation are powerful motives that have given evidence of their effectiveness," says Professor R. C. Kwant. "Never in history have such cogent motives been at work in favour of mutual understanding and unification."[19]

Positive co-operation—as has been said already—has become a real possibility also in virtue of the fact that the received Soviet system of dogma is being confronted by the course of history with such novel problems that the traditional ideology and its equally traditional interpretation no longer provide the answer; and this has given scope for some relatively independent thinking within the Communist camp.[20] Here is an aspect which the Christian must seize upon in his efforts to further the dialogue.

Correcting the distorted image

The Communists—not altogether without cause—have fashioned a caricature of Christianity. Christian candour constrains us to correct the distortions and the caricature of

Communism that are current in the Western world; for the view that we get of Communism is a warped one. We live under the proscriptive influence of a counter-propaganda that is inspired by the American press and backed by a considerable part of the West European press and is carried on against the Soviet Union. We have to remember that we are the victims of "hidden persuaders" who impose upon us, through the mass media, a particular image of Communism.

In the United States Communism has always been a "political issue"; and it is certain that the political bosses there have an interest in systematically keeping the fear of Communism on the go. This fear (which carries over on to the European scene) was at one juncture so intense that serious politicians were contemplating the possibility of a "preventive atomic war".

It is a commonplace of psychology that fear almost always distorts reality. American conflict-psychologists made an interesting study of the East–West conflict and reached some surprising conclusions.[21] The proclivity, in cases where there is never—or hardly ever—any personal contact, to attribute to people all sorts of bad or even monstrous characteristics, coupled with the tendency to mould reality into a logical unity and so to think in terms of simple opposites, has given rise on both sides of the East–West conflict to a stereotype of "the others" which is at a considerable remove from reality. Naturally, therefore, tourist encounters occasion a good deal of amazement; but they do not usually result in a definitive correction of the faulty stereotype. On its own ground, conflict-sociology comes to similar conclusions.[22]

The researches of these two new sciences only make one wonder just how much psychological and sociological subjectivity persists quite unnecessarily in the East–West conflict.

A comprehensive Christian social programme

It is a disquieting fact that Communism is successfully taking root in countries that are traditionally Catholic (or at any rate Christian). A rigid ecclesiasticism or the identification of Catholicism with a particular, established milieu or class is often the reason that an effective Christian social programme is lacking. If Communism alleges that religion alienates man from his true being as man by extinguishing in him every effectual desire to achieve a socially and economically well ordered world (the "opium"), we should not give the Communists any opportunity to substantiate this idea with facts.

An active, socially concerned Christianity, drawing its inspiration from religion, but well organized, too, from a human standpoint, must show the meaning of love for one's neighbour on a world scale. The Catholic Church ought to be giving a lead anywhere in the world where social injustice is occurring; and she must do this without hidden motives of proselytism. In a number of countries or areas of the world there is need for sociological studies designed to discover ways and means of detaching the Church from antiquated colonial or feudal systems with which in the course of centuries and in some territories (such as South America) she has come to be identified.

Special attention must be paid to the developing countries; and this should take the form more of a concern for the human being and less of a desire to introduce an ecclesiastical system beautifully structured from a canonical standpoint. A programme of social action on a global scale and deriving from an authentically Christian inspiration (the depth dimension) is part of the essential task of a true Catholicism.

A new study of Communism

There are already a fair number of systematic studies on the subject of Communism. In view of the new developments and of the new attitude—which is becoming more and more widespread—towards Communism, however, there is a pressing need for a fresh study of Communism as a phenomenon—and most especially where the Christian Churches are concerned.

As to the possibility of a dialogue—in the sense that we have in mind—this has never before been envisaged; and the absence of this element from the method of approach has produced a "blind spot" in every investigator, however thorough and scholarly he may have been. Thus a Protestant professor could declare, only a few years ago, that the real confrontation of Christianity and Communism has perhaps scarcely begun.

Scholars of the Reformed Churches in Germany are aiming, therefore, at a renewed study of Marxism *(Marxismus-Studien. Schriften der evangelischen Studiengemeinschaft,* Tübingen). The driving force behind these studies is the conviction that Marxism in its European form may be a seminal factor in the work of communicating the Gospel. Professor Banning discusses this in an article entitled: "Can Marxism still be relevant?" and answers as follows: "There is a process at work in which Christians are making the astonishing discovery that the basic starting-point of the young Marx may be fruitful. If so, it is possible to support the thesis that the real confrontation of Christianity and Marxism is only just beginning. That this process is going on in Germany, France and The Netherlands is more important than individual statements to the effect that 'it can't be, it ought not to be', and so forth."[23]

On the Catholic side also, Marxism is beginning to be studied in a new way. We have mentioned already the work of Professor Delfgauw in this connection. In a book that appeared recently yet another writer has pointed to the value of the Christian-Marxist confrontation:

Christianity has to learn specifically from Marxism that the present time makes special demands upon its peculiar ethic. One of the central points in that ethic is "love for the neighbour". Love is to be defined here as accepting, willing, supporting and furthering the subjectivity, selfhood, freedom of the other: But the subject that "the other" is is a subject in existence, a subject that is implicated in the world and that has to work itself up to its authentic being, in the world and upon it. Now the world in which the subject is implicated is not merely the world of nature but also the totality of economic, social and political structures that human history has thrown up. Because man is a subject-in-the-world, it makes no sense whatever for the Christian to claim to be loving his neighbour, unless his love finds its realization in opening the world to the neighbour and in making it accessible to him. But how is this to be done, save through economic, social and political activity? In so far as such economic, social and political structures as may exist render the world accessible to man, the Christian is in duty bound—at the imperative demand of Christian love—to reshape those structures.[24]

The one thing that these studies overlook is that contemporary Communism does not draw its basic inspiration solely from Marx. An investigation into the *fait primitif* on the basis of which modern Communism thinks and acts is an undertaking that would be much to the point and would fill in the gap.

So far as this goes, I have been gunning for the establishment of an institute or centre for experts who would study contemporary Communism with a view to confrontation and a possible dialogue. In odd places here and there some extremely important and useful work is being done in this sphere; but it all urgently requires co-ordination and that all the Christian Churches should work together at the international level (this too bears on the plan of a real Catholicism conceived as a task to be fulfilled). From an institute of this sort the initiatives for an active dialogue ought surely to come.

IV. The Actual Dialogue

If I am asked in what the actual dialogue consists, then I am bound to say that no one can form a concrete idea of it at this stage. I have tried to suggest what the new attitude is that should prevail on our side. A lot of traditional taboos and assumptions still have to be got rid of. Even so, one can already surmise, up to a point, what the stages of this dialogue are likely to be.

The first thing to aim at is an improvement in relations between East and West. On an optimistic view one might suppose that such an improvement is already—if only in a vague way—apparent. Where economic relations are concerned, progress is already on record. The economic situation in the world is such that by an intrinsic logic it is almost certain to lead to an increase in trade relations.

This development will demand of the Soviet Union and of the West some degree of adjustment of their economic structure. Eventually, the economic development will reach a point where any further advance is not really feasible without some corresponding political *entente* to ratify and support the links already established. It is then that East–West relations will enter the phase of political dialogue. The next step will be the cultural and scientific dialogue (although to a limited extent this exists already). As soon as this stage has been attained, the ideological dialogue will become possible.

Of course, this summary outline is not meant to suggest a chronological order of events. In practice, these various phases of the dialogue will interlock or overlap with one another. Nevertheless, I believe that this is the likely course of development and that the ideological discussion will come only at the end of it. This should not be allowed, however, to discourage us from making our preparations for that phase here and now.

There are many aspects of the dialogue with Communism that we have still not considered—and yet others that we have deliberately left on one side (such as Chinese Communism and its conflict with the Soviet Union). We might do well to remember that "the dialogue" has become more than ever a vital necessity for us, because the issue at stake is whether our civilization is to continue in existence or not. Thus it is by no means a question of a few simpletons riding their favourite hobby-horse in a state of ecumenical fuddle or intoxication. Rather ought we to say perhaps that the dialogue is an imperative Christian duty, in that the Christian is certainly called to make his contribution to the unification of mankind and to peace on earth.

Epilogue

About a month after the manuscript of this book had been completed the encyclical *Ecclesiam suam* appeared. It was a moving experience to feel justified in concluding that various ideas (or rather, aspirations) I had mooted had been given positive backing in this encyclical. I do not in any sense wish to "read back" anything into the encyclical or bend it to fit the standpoint I have adopted; but I may perhaps be allowed to point to certain notes sounded in *Ecclesiam suam* that are strikingly new.

New is the absence of the customary, somewhat inflated curial style; but the tone is modest too—a mixture of fatherly concern and love for the Church. Although the argument does not proceed explicitly from the "catholicity principle", the pope evidently wants to have done once and for all with everything that could hamper or constrict the universal mission of the Church. What is definitely thrown over is the idea of the Church as a closed group whose business it is to conserve and protect itself in a hostile world.

What the pope desires above all is a renewed awareness on our part of being the Church. He draws a distinction between "the ideal Church as Christ saw her" and "the Church as she has been and now is". As soon as the believer compares the Church as she has evolved through history with what that Church ought properly to be, "then there will grow up within the Church, of its own accord, an impatient longing for renewal". Therefore, "there rests upon the Church's shoulders today a duty to correct the faults of her own members". The springboard for all renewal is "that the Church of God should be as Christ willed her to be"—and that is not primarily a call upon the professional theologians to provide new theories about the Church; for "the mystery of the Church is not simply and solely an object of theological knowledge, but first and foremost a fact to be lived out". By this the Holy Father means to say that the theologians will make no advance in ecclesiology until our actually "being the Church" becomes something bigger and better than it is now. All the great questions regarding the Church "will find their solution through our experiencing the Church as a living reality".

Right through the encyclical there runs the thought that the Church of Christ must not be shut up in herself, but must order her life in terms of the mission that she has to the world. If she becomes rigidly set in ancient forms, the Church cannot carry out that mission. "In this altered world, with the Church in its midst, it is out of the question for the Church to adhere to the old ways." She must stand in the midst of modern life; and Christians should not hold themselves aloof but make themselves at home with all that is good in contemporary society, should "go along with this whole environment, clarify it, improve it, live in and through it and sanctify it. That—and nothing less—is the task facing the Church's members in this world."

Lastly, a great part of the encyclical is taken up with the "dialogue with the world"; for "the Church has a task in the world, which is: to proclaim the Gospel . . . and that means: to arrive at a dialogue . . . the Church wants to converse with everyone of good will".

Nobody, then, is to be left out. It is true that the pope is very cautious when speaking of the dialogue with atheists and particularly with atheistic Communism. Such a dialogue he regards as an extremely difficult undertaking; but he does add a further, explicit comment: "yet we do not exclude anyone out of hand, always provided that they are searching sincerely for the truth." And then there is a significant coda: "Pastoral considerations oblige us, however, to look for the psychological background, the causes of error and atheism. And then it will often appear that people have a false idea of God."

Others mentioned as partners in dialogue are: the Jews,

Islam and the religions of Africa and Asia. And then what is proposed is not simply a religious dialogue, but also that men should work together for "freedom of conscience, brotherhood and the ideals of social welfare and civic order". Special priority is given to the ecumenical dialogue and, finally, to what we have called the "interior catholicity" of the Church, the dialogue with the household of faith.

The pope is without doubt highly conscious of the dangers that the dialogue between Church and world must involve, and speaks at some length about them too; yet he is equally convinced that that dialogue is a vital necessity for the Church.

I admit that when it comes to declaring the Church's ills and shortcomings, both today and in the past, I have not beaten about the bush. This I decided upon, not in a carping or hostile spirit, but out of an honest regard for the Church. All too often a triumphalist attitude or a bogus spirituality has sought to hide the faults and errors of the Church. My intention, however, has been to offer as keen an analysis as possible of the Church's defects, so as to be able to see all the more clearly what are the points at issue in the Church, what things the Church at this moment of history is required to do. I believe, therefore, that I have not remained fixed in a purely negative posture.

I must leave the reader to judge whether or not I have made a modest contribution to a positive appraisal of what our being the Church involves.

Notes

INTRODUCTION

1. Treating theologically of the Church is something that has really been opened up only in the last few decades. Twenty-five years ago a theologian could write that ecclesiology was still in its pre-theological phase. See M. D. Koster, *Ekklesiologie im Werden* (1940).

CHAPTER I

1. See H. de Lubac, *Catholicism*, ch. II (London, 1950); also P. Rousselot and L. de Grandmaison, in *Christus* (1932), pp. 338–42.

2. Thus, for instance, M. Schmaus, *Katholische Dogmatik*, III, 1 (Munich, 1958), pp. 603–11.

3. Laurentius Klein, O.S.B., and Peter Meinhold, *Über Wesen und Gestalt der Kirche* (Freiburg, 1963), p. 53.

4. It is worth noting that Augustine, in one of his sermons, applies the parable of the leaven to the Church and her commission to express catholicity. Commenting on the words in the Gospel: "until the whole be leavened", he says: "By 'whole' we are to understand what the Greeks call *holon*. So long as you keep the bond of peace, you are at one with this whole, in the Greek, *katholon*. This is why the Church is described as Catholic" (*sermo* 3, 5: *P.L.*, 46, 828).

5. I am indebted for these thoughts to Professor A. Dondeyne. See his contribution in *L'Athéisme, tentation du monde, réveil des chrétiens?* (Paris, 1963), pp. 312–16.

CHAPTER II

1. Monasticism has sometimes had the character of a Christian élite.

2. A. Mirgeler, *Mutations of Western Christianity*.

3. G. van der Leeuw, *Balans van het Christendom* (Amsterdam, 1946), p. 25 f.

4. Textual compilation: A. Vermeersch, *De modernismo acta* (Bruges, 1908).

5. *Geschichte der Katholischen Kirche* (Berlin, 1953), p. 346.

6. For the history of modernism and integralism see: A. L. Lilley, *Modernism* (1908); J. Rivière, "Modernisme", in *Dictionnaire de Théologie Catholique*, X, col. 2009–47; R. Scherer, "Modernismus", in *Lexicon für Theologie und Kirche*, 7, col. 513–16; O. v. Nell-Breuning, "Integralismus", in *Lexikon für Theologie und Kirche*, 5, col. 717–18; G. Maron, "Reform-katholizismus", in *Die Religion in Geschichte und Gegenwart*, V, col. 896–903; Jos. Schmidlin, *Papstgeschichte der neuesten Zeit* (1934); A. Vidler, *The Modernist Movement in the Roman Church* (Cambridge, 1934); E. Hocedez, S.J., *Histoire de la Théologie*, III (Paris, 1947); *idem*, *Der Christ in der modernen Welt* (Cologne, 1955); H. Hermelink, *Das Christentum in der Menschheitsgeschichte*, III (Tübingen, 1955); Th. Schwegler,

"Rechts- und Linkskatholizismus", in *Schweizer Rundschau*, 59, (1959–60), pp. 417–26; *Au coeur de la crise moderniste*, ed. R. Marlé (Paris, 1960); E. Poulat, *Histoire du dogme et critique dans la crise moderniste* (Paris, 1962); primary sources for the history of the movement are the works of G. Tyrrell and F. von Hügel (esp. the letters, *Selected Letters* [1927]).

7. Of relevance here is the observation by the French philosopher, M. Merleau-Ponty: "At a time when Catholicism, especially in France, is penetrated by a movement of enquiry and research of considerable vigour —beside which the Modernism of the early part of the century looks sentimental and diffuse—the hierarchy is re-affirming, with the aid of the Syllabus, the most hackneyed forms of theological exposition." *Signes* (Paris, 1960), p. 307.

CHAPTER III

1. Heinrich Böll is a German Catholic novelist (satirist), of considerable repute and importance, whose books in Germany are widely read and many of which have been translated into English. *Ansichten eines Clowns* is his most recent book and was published in translation this year (London and New York) under the title, *The Clown*. All his fiction is firmly fixed in its social background; and different works satirize or expose various evils of contemporary society. His approach to his material is in some ways analogous to that of Brecht and a comparison with Dickens might also be made.

2. Gordon Zahn, *German Catholics and Hitler's Wars* (London and New York, 1965).

3. See also my article: "Kapitulatie van het Christendom", in *De Bazuin*, 46 (1963), 46/4.

4. H. Böll, *Hierzulande* (Munich, 1963), pp. 39–40.

5. C. Amery, *Die Kapitulation*, ch. IV (Reinbek, 1963); also E. W. Böckenförde, "Der deutsche Katholizismus im Jahre 1933", in *Hochland*, 1961; P. Weinburger "Kirche und Drittes Reich im Jahre 1933": *Werkhefte*, XII (April 1958), pp. 99 f.

6. Walter Dirks, "In Rom und in Fulda", in *Frankfurter Hefte*, 19 (1964), pp. 27–36.

7. R. C. Kwant, *De Fenomenologie van Merleau-Ponty* (Utrecht/Antwerp, 1962), pp. 168–70. See also: M. Merleau-Ponty, *Sens et non-sens* (Paris, 1948), pp. 305–21.

8. *Acta Apostolicae Sedis*, 29 (1937), p. 167.

CHAPTER IV

1. Hans Küng, in his inaugural lecture, "Das theologische Verständnis des Ökumenischen Konzils", pub. in *Tübinger Theologische Quartalschrift*, 141 (1961), pp. 50–7; later reproduced in a modified and extended form in the early chapters of *Strukturen der Kirche* (Freiburg, 1962); English translation: *Structures of the Church* (London, 1965 and New York, 1964).

2. *Structures of the Church*, p. 15 ff.

3. *Ibid.*, pp. 18–19.

4. *Catholica*, 15 (1961), 292–304.

5. *Stimmen der Zeit*, 87. 1 (1962), pp. 321–39.

6. Karl Rahner, *The Episcopate and the Primacy* (London and New

York, 1964). See also for this discussion: *Herder Korrespondenz*, 16 (1961/62), pp. 32 and 303.

7. See also the particularly interesting chapter, "The Charismatic Element in the Church", in Rahner's book *The Dynamic Element in the Church* (London and New York, 1964).

8. *The Dynamic Element in the Church*, p. 72.

9. *Ibid.*, p. 83.

10. I Sam. 3. 1.

CHAPTER V

1. *Hierzulande* (Munich, 1963), p. 23.

2. A somewhat compressed version of the original text.

3. In connection with this passage, see W. Luijpen, *Existentiële Fenomenologie* (Utrecht, 1959), pp. 267–79.

4. *Ibid.*, p. 271.

5. For this see the splendid articles by Professor W. K. Grossouw, "De moraal van de Bergrede" ("The ethics of the Sermon on the Mount") and "De twee geboden" ("The two commandments") in *Bijbelse Vroomheid* (Utrecht, 1955), pp. 49–80. Although written about eleven years ago, these expository essays still have no rival.

6. W. Luijpen, *Fenomenologie en Atheïsme* (Utrecht, 1963), pp. 198–203.

7. *Op. cit.*, p. 97.

8. Thus, for example, J. H. T. Robinson, *Honest to God*, (London, 1963), pp. 116–18.

9. *Ibid.*, p. 119.

10. W. van der Marck, O.P., "Vruchtbaarheidsregeling: poging tot antwoord op een nog open vraag" ("Control of reproduction: an attempted answer to a still open question"), in *Tijdschrift voor Theologie*, 3, (1963), pp. 378–413; J. M. Reuss, "Eheliche Hingabe und Zeugung, Ein Diskussionsbeitrag zu einem differenzierten Problem" ("Marital devotion and procreation. A contribution to the discussion of a complex problem"), in *Tübinger Theologische Quartalschrift*, 143 (1963), pp. 454–76; L. Janssens, "Morale conjugale et progestogènes", *Ephemerides theologicae Lovanienses*, 39 (1963), pp. 787–826; J. Rock, *The Time Has Come* (London and New York, 1963).

11. H. and L. Buelen-Gijsen, "Werkelijkheid en Formulering in de Huwelijksleer" ("Reality and the problem of formulas in the Doctrine of Marriage"), in *De Maand*, 7 (1964), p. 136.

12. This new structure in the Church was to a limited extent given practical expression in the United States when, in September 1963, a symposium was arranged on problems relating to population. It was organized by the Catholic University of Notre Dame; and among the participants were a number of theologians, sociologists, demographers and psychologists. The material was published in *The Problem of Population*, ed. Donald Barrett (University of Notre Dame Press, 1964).

13. Stanley Kutz, "Birth regulation in ecumenical perspective", in *The Ecumenist*, 2/4 (1964), pp. 57–9.

CHAPTER VI

1. I refer the reader to the very interesting inaugural lecture by Professor P. H. J. M. Camps, O.F.M., "In Christus verbonden met de godsdiensten der wereld" ("Christ—the link with the world's religions") (Utrecht/Nijmegen, 1964); copious references to the literature on the subject are to be found here.

2. This survey is largely derived from ch. 4, "Renewal of the Church, Past and Present", of the book by H. Küng, *The Council and Reunion* (London and New York, 1961).

3. J. Lescrauwaet, *Compendium van het Oecumenisme* (Roermond 1962), pp. 133–62. For the papal texts see G. Baum, O.S.A., *That they may be one: a study in papal doctrine Leo XIII—Pius XII* (London and New York, 1958).

4. J. Lescrauwaet, *op. cit.*, pp. 153–5.

5. What follows has been adapted from an article of mine, published in *De Volkskrant* for 28 March 1964 under the title: "Moeten Protestanten Katholiek worden?" ("Must Protestants become Catholics?").

6. In the light of what is said in this chapter the conciliar decree on Ecumenism is an extremely gratifying document. The very language of it is quite different from the phraseology traditionally employed in speaking of Protestantism. It is noteworthy that the expression "return to the one fold" nowhere occurs in the whole document. In many respects the contents of this decree exceed all expectations; and it gives grounds, therefore, for a large measure of ecumenical optimism.

7. J. Lescrauwaet, *op. cit.*, p. 174.

8. See, for instance, the issue of *De Protestant*, "Waar gaat het om? een brochure voor oecumenische discussie-clubs" ("What is at stake? A brochure for ecumenical discussion-groups"); it saddens one to read the account given of Catholic points of doctrine.

9. *Katholiek Archief*, 17 (1962), p. 511.

CHAPTER VII

1. *Geloof en Wereld* (Bilthoven, 1961), p. 177.

2. Pius IX in the encyclical *Qui pluribus* (1846) and in the *Syllabus* of 1864; Leo XIII in the encyclical *Quod apostolici muneris* (1878) and in *Rerum novarum* (1891); Pius XI in the allocution of 1924; encyclicals *Miserentissimus Redemptor* (1928); *Quadragesimo anno* (1931); *Caritate Christi* (1932); *Acerba animi* (1932); *Dilectissimi nobis* (1933); *Divini Redemptoris* (1937); Decree of the Holy Office (of 1949); condemnation of Chinese Communism in the encyclical *Ad Apostolorum principis* (1958).

3. In the encyclical *Divini Redemptoris, Acta Apostolicae Sedis*, 39 (1937), pp. 65–106.

4. *Nieuwe Eindhovense Krant* for 12 January 1963. Cf. also W. van Straten, *Zij noemen mij Spekpater*, pp. 75 and 76.

5. B. Delfgaauw in *De Maand* (August–September 1961); also in *De jonge Marx* (Baarn, 1962), pp. 119–26.

6. Professor Zacharias, O.F.M., in *De Bazuin*, 46 (1963), 35/1; and in *De Tijd* for 6 September 1963.

7. A. W. IJzerman, *Het moderne Kapitalisme* (1930), p. 278.

8. A particularly biased résumé can be found in *Documentation*, ed.

Institut Récherches de l'Europe Centrale (Louvain), 2, pp. 21–23, April 1963.

9. A. M. Knoll, *Katholische Kirche und scholastisches Naturrecht* (Vienna, 1962).

10. Cited by Rogier, *In Vrijheid herboren* ("Reborn to freedom"), p. 336.

11. Marx, in a contribution to the *Deutsch-Brüsseler Zeitung* for 12 September 1847; in: *Karl Marx/Friedrich Engels, Historisch-Kritische Gesamtausgabe*, 1, 6 (Frankfurt/Berlin, 1927), p. 278.

12. Paul Jostock, *Der deutsche Katholizismus und die Überwindung des Kapitalismus* (Regensburg, 1932), p. 138.

13. Tibor Kovács, *Het drama Hongarije* (Utrecht–Amsterdam, 1957), pp. 67 and 68.

14. See note 5.

15. See W. Luijpen, *Fenomenologie en Atheïsme* (Utrecht–Antwerp, (1963), pp. 198–203.

16. "Na tien jaar", *Wending*, 18 (1963), pp. 570–8.

17. Quoted in *Time*, vol. 83, no. 17 (1964), p. 21.

18. The phraseology and the ideas are taken from a very constructive article by Professor L. van Bladel: *Streven*, 16, vol. II, no. 8 (1963), pp. 765–72.

19. R. C. Kwant, "Het christelijke geweten en de bewapeningswedloop" ("The Christian Conscience and the Armaments Race"), in *Anti-revolutionaire Staatkunde*, 33 (1963), p. 140.

20. See, for example, the articles by H. Fleischer and D. D. Comey in *Studies in Soviet Thought*, vol. II, no. 4 (1962).

21. A write-up of the research appears in *The Journal of Social Issues*, 17, no. 3 (1961).

22. Cf. Doudt, De Moor, Thurlings and De Vooys, *Het conflict als maatschappelijk verschijnsel* ("Conflict as a Social Phenomenon") (Utrecht–Antwerp, 1962).

23. W. Banning, *Om mens en medemenselijkheid* ("For Man and his Shared Humanity") (Amsterdam, 1960), p. 101.

24. W. Luijpen, *op. cit.*, pp. 200 and 201.